SLOWING DOWN

"Sherry Welsh has uncovered the secret of slowing down to accelerate your career success . . . An entertaining and powerful book worth reading more than once!"

~ Steve Chandler
Author of *Time Warrior*

"A natural teacher with a big heart and a passion for helping others, Sherry Welsh has written a book that cuts to the heart of the matter behind female leaders' struggle to thrive: the failure to question their victim thinking and take ownership of their lives. With her no-nonsense approach, Sherry masterfully weaves together a rich tapestry of real stories, universal truths and powerful strategies to show us how to shift into slowed-down thinking, being and leading to create our most inspired, fulfilling, joy-filled lives!"

~ Melissa Ford
Entrepreneur and Professional Coach

SHERRY WELSH

SLOWING DOWN

UNEXPECTED WAYS TO THRIVE AS A FEMALE LEADER

B. C. Allen Publishing / Tonic Books

Slowing Down: Unexpected Ways to Thrive as a Female Leader

B. C. Allen Publishing/Tonic Books
Ben Allen
1500 SE Hawthorne Blvd
Portland, OR 97214

Contact the Publisher:
bcallenpublishing@gmail.com

Contact the Author:
www.sherrywelsh.com

Interior layout by Chris Nelson
Cover design by Dave Bricker

The Seven Levels of Energy chart used by permission of IPEC.

ISBN: 978-0-9968551-3-6

First Edition

To my Jonathon, for slowing me down enough to experience the joy, love, and laughter he brings to the world.

Acknowledgments

There are so many inspiring people who helped make this book possible. First and foremost is my son, Jonathon, who started telling people I was an author many years prior to this publication... He set the intention early on and I was motivated by his belief in me to make it happen! Next, Steve Chandler, life and business coach extraordinaire... without his guidance, inspiration and wisdom, I would still be holding back. To my literary coach, editor and publisher, Ben C. Allen... for his incredible gift for words, his vision, patience and sense of adventure... He made the process of becoming an author FUN! To my friends, clients and colleagues who helped me with their willingness to read and adjust the manuscript... they are Amanda Kertesz, Cynthia Hiskes, Melissa Ford, Leslie Sann, Tommy Spaulding, Lisa Prondzinski, Kelly Lyle, Andrea Hajciar, and Leslie Bednarz. To Jenny McKenna, Emily Welsh, and Connor O'Regan for their artistic insights. To my ex-husband, Tommy Hyman, who always supported me as a professional female throughout my career and who continues to share a common vision and a sense of humor about how we co-parent our son! To my parents, brothers and sister for teaching me so many life lessons along the way. Finally, to all my clients and colleagues, past and present, who have helped me slow down to see the world in a way that continues to expand and grow right before my eyes, all the while reminding me to slow dance with the universe.

Contents

I.

INTRODUCING THE SLOW LIFE

Chapter 1

Sharing What Works Best

This book is not meant to be a guide or another take on leadership. It is not a step-by-step instruction manual that will end with some uniform result. Like life, this book has no perfect recipe to follow.

This book is not an attempt to reinvent the wheel. The main purpose of this book is to share with you what has worked best for many of my clients, professional women at all levels in their career paths. This book is meant to help all women flourish.

In this book, I have integrated my own thoughts and practices with material from a variety of personal development coaches, leaders, and philosophers. I have developed an approach that helps female leaders to thrive.

Chapter 2

The Un-Slow Life aka Treadmill Living

"Speed is irrelevant if you are going
in the wrong direction."

~ Gandhi ~

Are you living the un-slow life? The treadmill life? Going through the motions? Always rushing toward the next goal, speeding through the weeks and months to get to the other side?

If you instantly understand what I mean, read on. But for those who do not understand, let me clarify. The image of the cartoon character George Jetson spinning on the treadmill, screaming, "Jane, stop this crazy thing" comes to mind.

Here's another way to describe it. Before I dove headfirst into personal development, I was a success in many regards. A wonderful son, a high paying job, and a beautiful house. I traveled the world, ate at amazing restaurants, and worked with incredible people in many different countries. Life was amazing, and I am deeply grateful for all the opportunities that I was given.

Even with all that, something was not right. I was actually living the treadmill life. And running full speed! I was rushing toward something 'out there,' something to help me feel more complete. Below the surface of success, a vital element was missing. I couldn't name what it was, but I certainly could feel its absence. And this created in me a deep searching that turned into the fast dash forward to that next shiny thing.

I was moving at such a breakneck pace that I couldn't see how I was missing the mark. Let alone attain the element to feel completion. When I reflect back on those times now, when I slow down the memory tapes and take a look at what was really going on, a different picture comes into focus. A picture that reveals a more complex image than my surface success.

It was a time of great achievement, but I was never able to savor it. In my haste, I was rushing by all these wonderful things so fast they became a blur. The treadmill was set to a sprint, and I kept passing the world by.

Let me show you what the treadmill life looked like up close...

I wanted a rewarding career and was willing to do whatever it took to keep progressing but, at the same time, I was wanting to spend more time with my son, my friends, and even for myself. My focus was split. I was driven to succeed in this environment, while nurturing loving relationships with others and taking time to nurture myself. And I wasn't able to do it all, because I prioritized the headlong rush for more success.

As I traveled the world, it felt like I never really landed. Often I missed my family. I focused on the next trip, the next week or month, eager to be finished with the current one. Traveling became a chore. In each new place I became restless. I would eagerly await my breaks from the constant flights and flashing lights of foreign cities. My bed at home and my family were a distant refuge I rarely knew. In their place was a half sleep on an overnight flight or the bleached sheets of another hotel room. After twenty years of traveling, the glamour lost all its shine.

I am still friends with many of the talented people I worked with, but while I was full stride in the treadmill life, I rarely slowed down to enjoy the time together. This put me at odds with one of my core values—connection with others. We'd see each other face to face, but I felt like I had one foot out the door. This was not genuine connection. The connection between us was obstructed.

I often passed through my beautiful home like an object on a conveyor belt. I'd stop in, unpack, do laundry, repack, rush back out the door. Bing, bang, boom. I took for granted the warmth and openness of the space I now call "home." The careful, nuanced work of the builder was lost on me. I was never "home." I was only "back". It was subtle but clear that I didn't feel like I belonged there.

People would compliment me on my outward success, and I at times would feel fleeting bits of happiness with this, and, yet, internally, there was this voice of judgment that said, "You aren't doing enough. You need to do more."

As I continued to get promoted and as I continued to have my responsibilities expanded, it was not easy much of the time, because I felt like a phony in so many ways. As one of the few women in male-dominated firms, I believed that to succeed and fit in I had to be one of the boys. I had to act like them, think like them, talk like them, drink like them... etc. Many days I was exhausted doing this. When I look back, I can see that I had felt like I was wearing a mask throughout the day restricting my natural feminine energy. I can see now how this put me at odds with myself and how there was a subtle voice of self-judgment that said my feminine qualities had to be denied. This denial, for any woman who knows, puts a woman out of alignment, and is exhausting. A part of me was denied and pushed back into a corner.

It sounds like I regret much of my life; I assure you that I don't! What I reminisce about is being able to see now what joy I seemed to have missed as I rushed by it all. I would love to savor those moments in my past. And this reminds me that today is a new day. From this moment forward, every day I practice intentionally slowing down and enjoying each moment with every person wherever I am. To rephrase Steve Hardison, the Ultimate Coach, I only focus on one person at a time, the person I'm with in this moment. And sometimes that person is me.

While sped up, I was directed toward a type of success, and was overlooking what would actually bring me happiness. The hidden beliefs that were driving me disconnected me from the present moment.

Chapter 3

Other Hidden Troubles with the Un-slow Life

When you're living the un-slow life, you're living for the future, living for some goal up ahead that you will never reach. And in this way, you are putting yourself at odds with the present, which only strips more power from you. Happiness and fulfillment become delayed. Unattainable. Stranded out there in the foreign future.

Accordingly, burnout occurs. The more stress and less fulfillment that comes with this way of life, the harder the treadmill runner will push herself to get to that distant future and the relief it brings.

In this state, it's easy to struggle with others, too, which of course makes life harder and happiness feel even further away. Frequently, you fight with co-workers, children, parents, siblings, and bosses. Then you may find yourself harboring resentments for anyone that slows your headlong rush toward future success and the happiness associated with it. When unmanaged, these brushes with others, then, can turn into sores and lingering wounds that worsen with time.

In the treadmill life, there is no time to slow down and handle the present. There is no time to relax when serenity and peace and success are so far off. Fearful questions and disempowering beliefs lodge at the back of the mind, unconsciously urging for more action. Even the thought of changing our approach to life seems scary and holds us hostage.

"What would I be, if I weren't living this

way? Would I still achieve my goals?"

"What will happen if I actually change my approach to life? Will I want to leave my job or my partner? Will my partner want to leave me? And then what? What if I actually find happiness? Some of us even have this question lurking around, a question that creates so much discomfort it compels us to dive deeper into the distraction of more work: "Do I even deserve success?"

Truth be told, when I began learning to slow down, I did see that there was a lot I had to address. I learned that much of my trouble came from the way I related to the world and the beliefs that I held about the world and the people in it. I learned that I was trying to fit into a corporate culture using character traits that didn't suit me or feel good to me. I was living someone else's notion of success and happiness.

Simply put, I believed I was at the mercy of the world and the people around me. I didn't see that I actually had many choices. I didn't see how I could really question and challenge my beliefs. How I could shift the way I was seeing the world.

And I then began to discover that happiness is already inside me... it was just covered up by all the beliefs I had piled on over many years that led me down the path of believing it was somewhere else.

This discovery of the slowed down life, the digging into the present moment to find happiness, true success, and freedom—that is the point of this book. To reveal to you the ways that happiness and joy and ownership have entered my life and the lives of my clients as a result of slowing down, questioning beliefs to gain clarity, moving from a place of victimhood to empowerment, and ultimately finding that state of peace and fulfillment that I know exists in us all.

II.

SLOWING DOWN: FROM CONFLICT TO COLLABORATION

Chapter 4

Frustrated Mandy

Tension knotted Mandy's forehead and tightened her joints. She sat stiffly in the chair like a rigid metal bolt, and I knew that we needed to dial this frustration down before any progress could be made. Mandy had come to our session frustrated with a peer who was aggressive and insulting to her and her team.

Mandy was falling into a common pitfall. When we think *only* of ways to take back whatever power we think was stolen from us, we impair our ability to see what is actually happening, which keeps everyone in the relationship stuck. When we focus just on the seeming injury, we overlook every other part of the interaction.

Mandy started to explain her situation. "We have this woman in our company who is really mean. She sends insulting e-mails, is always putting others down, and is destroying my team's morale."

"How often do you interface with her, and in what areas?" I asked.

"She is one of the managers of another department and we, as Recruiting and Talent Management, provide service to her and her team to fill open positions. We have to interact a lot."

"Give me an example of how she communicates in a destructive manner. We'll work on that example."

By looking at a specific example, we can slow down the feelings and seduction of anger and start making actual discoveries about what is causing those feelings. When someone's only allowing their anger to distort their interpretation of an event, they overlook many of the details of the exchange in order to prove they're right and validate their need to nurse their indignation.

"OK... just this morning she sent an email describing how slow my team is to respond to her needs, how incompetent an associate on my team is, and how she needs to do all the work to fill this open position," Mandy said with a sting of pain in her voice. "She said she doesn't even know why my department exists."

"Wow... OK... here's a great opportunity to practice opening up and truly listening to her! It sounds like she doesn't feel heard. It sounds like she is frustrated because the position she has open is not yet filled and that is creating stress, compromising her ability to do her job well. It's also compromising her team's ability to perform well when there is work to be done by someone that is not there."

"Well, yes, I'm sure it is difficult for her team to meet their objectives when someone is missing. But she doesn't have to be so mean about it!"

"I agree. And when anyone is critical or insulting or frustrated with you or your team, their feelings are more about something going on within them than they are about anything you've done or haven't done," I said, slowing down my voice to help de-escalate her feelings. "So what else do you believe may be going on with her that is fueling her aggression toward your team?"

"Well, I know her boss recently resigned, and she has a new one that none of us know anything about..." The sharpness of anger in Mandy's voice was beginning to dull. "Her previous boss was the one that brought her into the company."

"So what do you think is going on in her head right now about her job security?"

"Oh..." Mandy said with a bit of softness in her voice. "I hadn't thought about that. She's probably scared that she has to start from scratch to build a new relationship with her new boss... She's probably not sure whether the new boss will want to bring in his own guy for her job."

"Yes! That happens all the time!" I said. "It doesn't mean it will this time, but it could be one possibility that she's afraid of. So how might you be able to help her with some of that fear?" I wanted Mandy to focus on helping rather than blaming. In this way, she would transform her anger and create a more meaningful relationship with this co-worker, one with a true sense of caring and collaboration. Even if Mandy kept this intention totally silent within her, it would relax her attitude toward her colleague and take her out of the trenches of defense that had embittered her.

She wanted to take it further. "Well, I could sit down with her and ask her how it's going with the new boss and see what comes up. Then I could recommend some ways for us to communicate more effectively that would help both of us do our jobs better."

"I love it! When are you going to sit down with her?"

"I will send her a meeting invite after this session."

That's exactly what she did. She developed ways to help her colleague, to patch up their past negative interactions, and to establish better communication practices so they wouldn't fall into the same pattern again. She chose bravery over fear and pain. She chose ownership over victimhood. She chose the slowed down route to clarity, communication and better living.

Chapter 5

Acknowledge and Validate

A skill I introduce to clients that helps them shift themselves and others out of Victimhood into a more productive state is *Acknowledge and Validate.* Acknowledge and Validate is an important practice that encourages someone to empathetically consider the other person's fears and concerns. This creates a sense of common ground, so that any actions and conversations can take place from this place of understanding. When we take time to seek another's perspective it helps to release the grip of anger and the sense of injury that one may feel.

Using this skill requires you to actively listen. Be fully present. Listen intuitively for what's not being said and listen for what beliefs your colleague, spouse, child, or friend may have that has them feeling helpless or angry.

When using "Acknowledge and Validate" to shift from conflict to collaboration, the first step is to be fully focused on what's going on for the other person. Be open-minded. Allow them to share with you everything that is going on that led them to Victim Land. The next step is to acknowledge what they are feeling (frustrated, helpless, angry) based on what they've said. Next, validate their feelings as being totally understandable given what they just shared with you. Genuinely let them know it makes sense they feel the way they do. This doesn't mean you have to agree with them or that you would feel the same way they do. It simply means that you truly can see that given what they are believing in the moment, it's totally understandable they feel the way they do. Finally, to move them into a more collaborative state, ask them how you can support them, what can you do to help them take action to move forward with the task, assignment, activity, etc. This is a powerful skill that, when practiced, becomes a natural way of being and a surefire way to move yourself and others into a more productive space.

Chapter 6

Anger is Fear

When we're cramped up by our anger and indignation, the energy we have to help those around us and help us make a difference in the world is cramped up too. The energy gets tied up in a nonproductive cycle. Instead of flowing through us, it gets lodged inside of us in the form of agitation and fixation on how we were wronged. This is a cycle of self-obsession in which we keep reliving the injury over and over again. Thus, we let ourselves become distracted by resentment, which diminishes our ability to be effective in other areas of our lives, and further mangles our relationships.

When we are angry or tense, we operate in what is called a catabolic state, one which is draining, exhausting. Stress and worry, too, are catabolic states. As humans, we fluctuate between catabolic states and their counterpart, anabolic states, which are inspiring and productive. Once we start to gain awareness into the ways we shift between these states and slow down the automatic functions that lead us between them, then we begin to take more ownership in our lives.

With anger, when we step back from the situation, and when we dare to get outside of our own hurt for a moment, we can start to see what's truly going on in our interactions with others. Whenever two people are in conflict, one has seemingly threatened the other as a result of some unmanaged fear. Fear is always the heart of the conflict. And this understanding alone will help us move into a more compassionate, anabolic state.

Trouble with coworkers is often a huge struggle for my clients (and for people generally), and it can cause tremendous problems within a company. In its slightest form, it lingers in the office like a bad smell. At its worst, it can undermine the success of entire companies. Most of the time, it just builds up and ebbs, builds up and ebbs, or just builds till a breaking point is reached, at which point something or someone inevitably explodes in anger or resentment. To be happy at work, and coincidentally most effective and productive, we must question our beliefs about our coworkers and our interactions with them as they appear in the moment. When we question the beliefs that lead to conflict with coworkers, we can practice greater empathy and therefore soothe ourselves, quieting the static and the noise inside.

How does this transition from conflict to empathy start? It's simple.

We slow down to question our beliefs to see if there isn't another way of looking at the situation. We acknowledge and validate the other person so they can feel truly heard. Then, we develop an action plan together that will lead to success. This is the course Mandy and I took, and her story vividly shows how slowing down can construct powerful relationships.

Chapter 7

Finding Your Voice

I was in my first job out of college. The year was 1986, and I was earning 5 dollars an hour, no thanks to the engineering degree my father talked me into. I was in a junior role as a cost estimator for a manufacturing firm, because I didn't go the traditional route and get an internship in my field. Engineering didn't call to me, really. Nor did this job. I felt underpaid, and not passionate at all in the work I was doing, so when the man I had been dating asked me to go south to Florida with him, it was an easy choice to leave the company.

I was fed up feeling underpaid and under-valued. And besides... I was in love!

I knew the president of the company, who was a family friend, and I went into his office to have a talk with him. I sat in front of his desk. The sky was over his shoulder in a partially opened window; it was midday and bright. I told him my decision to leave, that I was moving to Florida with Bill (who also worked for him). That I was ready to move on.

He was shocked to hear all this. He asked me why I would leave when I was just getting my career started. "Well," I said, a little bitter and a little timid, "You never paid me very much. I only got 5 dollars an hour!"

His look of shock became tinged with confusion, as he leaned forward in his chair a little to look me in the eye.

"Well, Sherry. You never spoke up. You never asked for any more. If you didn't think you were worth more than 5 dollars an hour enough to ask for it, then why should I think you're worth more than 5 dollars an hour?"

This response struck me at my core. Except for the dull sound of a passing car, the room was quiet.

I paused and just stared back at him. I hadn't realized that I could ask for a raise, that, if I thought I deserved it, I *should* ask for a raise. Even if it felt uncomfortable, it was my responsibility to step up and ask for what I wanted. Who else, after all, will do the speaking for me?

I left his office that day and never went back. But that lesson has stayed with me forever. It has shaped my evolution as a person and employee. That's not to say he made it easier for me to ask for what I want or deserve, but his comments put a fire in me and drove me to keep practicing this vital skill.

Over the years, I have learned appropriate, professional ways to do this, which may, oddly enough, include saying "no" when appropriate and setting clear boundaries. I have learned that when I ask for what I want and deserve, I'm healthier *and* the company is healthier, too. This is a true win-win.

For anyone who wants to take his or her life and career to the next level, they must absolutely develop this skill. Most companies will not simply anticipate what you want, and then lay it all out for you on a silver platter. You may not truly appreciate what they give you if you don't have to ask for it. And they may even give you something you don't really want. Being clear and communicating openly about what works for you or doesn't work for you benefits everyone involved!

When I chose to leave a British cosmetic packaging firm to start my coaching career, I was offered a severance package that was good, but didn't send me off with what I needed for my transition through the start of my own business. I had worked hard for them over the two years I was there, and we had helped the company to improve and grow. The business had grown partly as a result of the improved customer service approach we put in place. I had an honest look at what I had implemented and the value it created for them. I asked for what I deserved. It took guts. But it was vital to my family, my new business, and me.

When it was time for me to ask, I realized that the worst that could happen is that they would say no. That had happened to me before when I lost my job in the auto industry during a recession. Even when I had not gotten what I asked for then, I was still okay. I figured it out. I actually ended up doing even better than in previous years!

In my personal life, too, I have learned to ask for what I want. When I was going through my divorce, I wrote out my vision for a co-parenting relationship with my ex-husband. This was the most productive way for me to get clarity on what I really wanted, what I believed would be best for my son, my ex-husband, and me. So I put it in a letter to him and we talked through it.

Ten years later, we are living the way we talked about. And we're good friends, even. We support each other as it relates to our time with our son, respect each other and our individual lives, and are loving role models for our son. Many of my friends have commented over the years how well we get along and what a model divorce we have (if there is such a thing). I smile when I hear that as I remember it coming back to what I asked for.

There was no room for unspoken expectations of what was going to happen after the divorce. We had talked through it together with always the focus on what would be best for our son given the fact he would be going back and forth between two households.

Resentment and frustration can build when there are unspoken expectations of what "should" happen. We avoided much of that by each of us asking for what we wanted and being willing to talk it through, adjusting as the years unfolded.

Chapter 8

Professional Self

Leslie came to a session with the complaint that she kept getting heaps of work, without getting any recognition or promotion along with them. When Leslie inquired about getting promoted, her boss continued to tell her that she needed to "prove herself" before moving to the next level.

You can imagine her concerns about this, and the resulting problems it created. The harder she worked, the more exhausted she became. The more exhausted she became, the harder she had to work. As this cycle took hold of her life, her boss still did not give her the recognition she desired, and so she felt even more frustrated and defeated.

By the time Leslie came to me, she was exacerbated and resentful. She thought she had been doing everything right and expected to be given a raise by that time for being such a good worker. No matter how much more she did, that raise never came, and it seemed her boss's requirements only grew each day. Frustration built. Then resentment. She told me that she hates to go to work.

In our coaching session, my first goal was to slow her down, so we could digest this situation in bite-sized chunks, and eventually get at the pith of the issue. Once there, we had to get her into a state of ownership over the problems she faced. These situations were not happening *to* her; they were happening in part *because of* her. I wanted her to see the ways in which she was enabling her boss to overlook her need for recognition.

"What do you really want out of this whole situation? What is ideal?" I asked her, trying to get a sense of what we could work toward in our session.

"Well," Leslie said, "I want my career to continue to progress. I want additional responsibilities, a higher-level title, better pay, and the perks that go along with these. But instead, I keep getting additional work given to me. And no title."

"Tell me what's currently in your way of requesting that from your boss?" I asked with the intention of helping her into an ownership role. I wanted her to see that even though this situation felt out of control, her beliefs and actions (or inactions) created her frustration and perpetuated this situation.

"I shouldn't have to request it," she interjected. "They should realize how much more I'm doing and then proactively take care of it." I could feel the pent-up tension spilling out in her voice. She had been giving so much and felt like she was being treated unfairly. She was at the point where she couldn't give anymore without getting the recognition she had been working hard to achieve.

"I'm sorry to be the bearer of bad news, Leslie," I said firmly but sympathetically. "It doesn't work like that. You have to ask for what you want in life... all aspects of life. How can your boss give you something different if he doesn't know what you want? How can he know what you want if you don't tell him?"

"But I have told my boss what I'm looking for career-wise last year when we sat down and did my performance review."

"Great! So given what you last discussed with him, what have you done to update him on the progress you've made toward the goals you both agreed upon?" I said again nudging her to take ownership of the present moment rather than relying on an action that is stranded in the past, out of her reach.

"Well, I haven't done anything formal; I just keep being a great team player and taking on more work when asked."

"Can you see how that doesn't work for you, Leslie?" I asked. "You see that staying quiet doesn't serve you, nor does it fulfill the agreement you made, right?"

She nodded.

"It's actually a bit of a paradox," I continued. "When you don't say anything about what you need, then continue to take on an additional workload, you actually perform worse with your basic tasks and you look like you're a 'not-meeting-expectations-type' associate, instead of the great team player that is taking on more than expected. Your desires to get a promotion and take on more responsibilities are overlooked when you just quietly take on more responsibilities and wait to be noticed."

"Yes! That's exactly what's been happening! What can I do about it without looking like a complainer and a weak associate?"

Her questions were shifting into ownership questions, which you can almost always identify by the words, 'What can I do?'

"You can have your Professional Self kick in here," I suggested. "Regardless of your next performance review, you can invite your boss to a meeting. Then update him on what goals have been accomplished so far this year. You can tell him what additional work has been done that was above and beyond the core role you're filling."

"Yes! Then I can ask for the promotion."

"That's one option," I responded. "Another might be that you go in without any expected outcome. That way you can create a new agreement on what your career timing looks like for the next year. He may have even better ideas than just the next level increase for you!" If she went into the meeting with just one idea in mind, she might close off other options. Whereas, going in with an open mind could lead to more collaborative visions for her future. Better ones, perhaps.

"Yes! He might even want me to take an overseas assignment. That'd be awesome!"

In our conversation, Leslie started with her feelings of being overwhelmed, burdened, frustrated, and overlooked. When she slowed down and took a look at how she had a part in creating this situation, she was able to move from a state of victimhood to a state of ownership. From there, she was able to make decisions and take actions that would help her build the future she wanted. She could abandon the frustration. As she developed concrete steps to act on immediately, she felt more satisfied and empowered to build the life she wanted now.

Chapter 9

Getting Clarity: Pleasing the Boss's Boss

Amanda was just three weeks into her new job when she came to see me, and she was already stressed out of her mind. She didn't know yet if she had to pull together information for a meeting with her boss's boss the following week, and she was spiraling out of control as her overwhelm threatened to shut her down.

She couldn't think straight, speak up, or focus. A former boss of mine, would have put it in her usual blunt way—"She's getting her panties all tied up in a bunch."

She had tied herself up in a knot of anxiety and fear, and she couldn't function. Failure for her felt imminent. That only made it all worse.

Amanda, like so many of us, wanted to please her boss and her boss's boss. She wanted to be the newest glowing success in the office and she wanted this gratification immediately, less than a month into her new job. In car lingo, she wanted to go from 0 to 60 in 2.5 seconds. But this desire to move at absurd speeds was causing her to suffer and, worse, potentially crash and burn. Amanda had to do what often feels counterintuitive: she had to slow down.

"I am totally stressed out about this meeting coming up on Monday," she blurted out in her tense voice. "My boss normally leads it, but she's out sick. I'm just not sure what I'm supposed to do... Do I lead the meeting? What am I supposed to prepare and give to her boss? What will be useful?"

"OK..." I said slowing down the pace of my words a

little. "Take a breath."

"OK." Her eyes were starting to glisten with tears.

"Of course you're overwhelmed... you're used to being a high performer, and after three weeks in this big company, you're thinking you should have it all figured out by now... it totally makes sense that you're frustrated and exhausted..."

"Yes! My boss is out sick so I can't ask her any questions. I don't know whether or not she wants me to take her place in this meeting with her boss and the other executives. I have no idea what is involved. I don't want to look incompetent in front of them all." Amanda would pause and look around as if the answer to her struggle was drifting through the air over my shoulder. "I am thinking I can pull together some slides, but I'm not sure if that is a good idea...." She kept adjusting and readjusting herself in the chair.

"OK... wow... I can see the struggle..." I said with a noisy exhale. "I'm even feeling exhausted hearing all the things you're mentally juggling. That is so much to try and anticipate and adjust to without guidance. You don't even know if you're supposed to lead the meeting or what to present if you are leading it... I can see the worry."

"Yes, but I want to look like I know what I'm doing. And I want to be proactive."

"I get that. I love that you are proactive," I said before a slight pause. "But only when it makes sense and is valuable for yourself and others..." I paused again to see if she was warming up to this line of thinking. "So let's break this down and see where you can begin. What is the first meeting on Monday that you want to get prepared for?"

I wanted her to pull something specific from the web of thoughts that she was tangled in. This is designed to help slow her thinking down, so that the thoughts become manageable, which puts her back into a state of ownership.

"The European Market review."

"OK. Tell me who leads the meeting?"

"My boss's boss."

"OK. Has your boss asked you to be her proxy in the meeting since she is out sick?"

"No. But she might."

"Yes, she 'might.' But it's not very effective and productive to plan your day around 'mights'."

"But I want to be prepared in case she does."

"So, what can you do to find out whether or not you will be the proxy for your boss?" I asked, wanting to give her an empowering question so she could get moving and take control of her life in this situation, rather than stress out while waiting for others to give direction.

"I can ask her."

"YES! And what else will you ask her when you speak with her next?"

"I will ask her what specifically she wants me to have prepared for the meeting."

"What else?"

"I'm not sure."

"Well, how about if you ask her what she recommends for you to do to connect with her boss, the leader of the meeting? Ask her if you can do anything prior to Monday to ensure that what you prepare is relevant and useful."

"Yes! And I can take advantage of the time with her to get to know her better since I rarely get the chance to interact in that way with her or with people at her level in the company."

"I love it!"

As we continued to talk about her desire to look like she knew what she was doing (after only three weeks), the desire to please her boss, the desire to be high-performing in this role as quickly as possible, and the desire to feel like she mattered in her new job, she realized that she was already doing the best she could. This allowed her to take more pride in how far she'd come and to relax. When relaxed, she could perform at her optimal level.

She also realized that she hadn't asked for clarity on what tasks lay before her, before she'd started spinning out of control. If she had been clear on her boss's (and her boss's boss's) expectations, then she would have known exactly where to apply her energy and what to focus on. This, too, would not only have helped her feel better, it would've helped her perform at her highest level and provided exactly what the company needed in that moment. The uncertainty of not knowing what to do agitated her fears. It allowed overwhelming thoughts and feelings to sweep in and hold her hostage.

I completely understood Amanda's plight, so it was an amazing gift to revisit these ideas with her. So many times in my past I, too, had wanted to prove my usefulness to a new boss. And during those times, I felt like I never had a moment to spare. I was rushing everywhere, managing everything, and not simply slowing down and asking what would be most useful.

When I consider the desire to prove myself immediately, I can see that it comes from a simple, and very natural fear. I had felt insecure in my new job and new surroundings, so I wanted to find security as quickly as I could. I wanted to make sure my new boss felt reassured that he or she had made the right choice when I was hired. I also wanted to prove to myself that I could do the job and do it well. And I didn't want to be rejected or lose my position after it took me so long to find it!

Knowing this, it was easy to identify that—in

moments like the one Amanda described—my boss hadn't rejected me, and I hadn't lost my job. I had merely been trying to figure out what action was right in that moment. I feared losing my job and being fired, but that is just because I kept telling myself in my head that I would be let go if I didn't perform a certain way, and that I had to figure out fast what that "way" was. I kept telling myself these damaging stories about failure that weren't based on reality but on my own insecurities. They seemed real to me, just as they seemed real to Amanda. And so they caused feelings of being overwhelmed to the point that I didn't know what move to make next.

But when I questioned the validity of those types of stories and started to ask instead what I could do in the moment, I moved into a place of clarity and empowerment. From there, I could make progress. From there, I could make an impact. From there, I could stop all the spinning, and find my footing. From there, calm and balanced, I could be the leader I was needed to be.

Chapter 10

Fear, Worry, Anxiety—Oh, My!

"I am an old man and have known a great many
troubles, but most of them have never happened."

~ Unknown Author ~

Even just hearing the word "fear" makes me tense. My insides start to knot. I begin to shut down and withdraw deeper into myself. That physiological response is evidence of my victim mode kicking in. In these states, the fight or flight response activates inside me. Or, perhaps, fear causes me to completely freeze up, leaving me incapacitated. Unable to take action in any direction. And imagine – fear is something we create. It is formed from simple thoughts in our head!

I find it no wonder we have these thoughts; fear is all around us, in almost every aspect of our multi-media culture. It is in news reports, magazines, articles, television shows, etc. Each of these mediums continually reports stories that instill some type of fear or distrust or doomed outlook in its viewer or listener, views that often lead to actions that only exacerbate whatever fears comes up. Fear is what makes people become hostile or distrusting toward others. It makes us greedy and paranoid, clouded by our judgment of those around us.

The media, it seems, loves provoking hostile feelings, fear, or even sadness in its audience. These

35

emotions then rile up viewers, and riled viewers pay close attention, watch more, and watch often. They feed the monster of fear that's been created. Rarely do I turn on the news to hear about the loving thing a husband did for his wife that morning. Seldom does the news report on the way someone took it upon herself to help another person overcome a huge struggle. On occasion we hear how a child has started a charity. But along with this inspiring story, we're given the sense that those acts of altruism and kindness are rare in an otherwise hostile, cold, tough world.

With these social influences all around us, I find that I spend much of my time with clients working on conquering their biggest fears. They are bombarded with fearful attitudes and, like most people, my clients are well-versed in telling themselves disempowering stories about what's available to them in the world. Pain and trouble. And more pain. The time we work together is, in part, meant to help them move past these fears. Our goal is to bring the fears out of hiding, put them on the table for inspection. Then we can question and disassemble them so that they vanish forever! By letting go of our belief in a fear, it takes away the power the fear holds over us, making it much harder for that fear to materialize again in our lives.

From the many sessions I've had with high-performing women about their fears, I've compiled a list of the most common fears:

1. Fear of not being able to do it or have it "all"
2. Fear of failing as a mom while having a career
3. Fear of regret—missing their kids' growing up
4. Fear of losing control
5. Fear of money—too much or too little
6. Even fear of success!

No matter the kind of fear, the methods for overcoming them are the same. Bring the fear into the light and examine it for the inherent flaws in its makeup. Acknowledge what about this fear is not true, what is based on some false belief. Then allow the fear to vanish. In the following section, you will see how this works. A client of mine, was kind enough to allow me to share her experience here with you.

Chapter 11

The Fear Symphony

Shortly into our session, Molly told me that she loved her job and didn't want to leave it.

"But I don't think I can have it all," she continued. I could see the torment in her face as she spoke. "I am committed to my job and the position I hold there. I've worked so hard to get to where I am, and I don't want to give it up; I love it! But I miss so much time with my children."

Molly works late and never gets to pick her kids up from school "like the other moms do." She is attentive and caring in many regards, but she feels so much guilt about her interest in her job and believes that it pulls her away from being present with her children as they grow up.

She showed this internal conflict even in the way she rapidly shifted between topics. She would talk about her guilt, then immediately mention something about the job that she loved, like her latest project. She described with passion how incredible it felt to win new business with a customer that had sworn off her company due to a major quality issue in the past. I could see her light up and go into more details about the big win, rising slightly from her chair as if elevated by the memory of this validating experience.

Then, moments later, after briefly relishing in the victory, she would get sullen again. "I guess I just have to give it up and make time for my kids right now." Her guilt was palpable, and she shrunk down in her chair like a punished toddler. "They are only young for a short time, and I don't want to miss it. I'm afraid I'll screw them up by not being around enough." I nodded quietly, listening to her, caring for her, and thinking, *Perfect. We have lots to work with in this session!*

For Molly, several fears were coming together to create the guilt she felt burdened with. Fear #1 (fear of not being able to do it all) began to encompass Fear #2 (fear of failing as a mom), Fear #3 (fear of regret), Fear #4 (fear of losing control of her life and her kids' lives), Fear #5 (fear of money, or losing it if she stepped away from her career), and yes, even Fear #6 (fear of Success)! I mean, what would the other moms say about her being successful in her career and "missing" time with her kids?

Molly's fears were like elements of a symphony all coming together to create a giant, discordant nail-biting concert of anxiety. And we were in the thick of a crescendo! Our job then was to start muting certain instruments. As we started questioning each of her fears, Molly began seeing the truth about what she believed. As she started to ease up and relax, the volume of each fear began subsiding, even if only slightly.

We began simply, by exploring her definition of the word "all." If Molly was afraid of not being able to have it "all", I wanted to help her articulate exactly what that meant to her. "All" means something different to each and every one of us, and I wanted to make sure she wasn't falling into the trap of using the media's definition, or borrowing some definition from someone in her past. When we got down to it, for Molly, "all" meant having a thriving, rewarding career that continued to progress *and* raising two kids full-time *and* taking care of her husband *and* being the caregiver for her aging father *and* volunteering as a mentor in the Big Brother/Big Sister program. Even as she listed each of these items that she truly expected herself to fulfill, she seemed a bit exasperated.

I smiled and said, "So is that all?"

She laughed.

We then began to slow down, and look at how her desire to be a caregiver was dominating her life. She wanted to take care of everyone close to her and have a fully rewarding career. This desire to help is great when used in authentic service for others, but there is one guiding rule that shouldn't be forgotten. The ones providing service should not overextend their service; the service should be done in the spirit of reaching a win-win outcome. When we forget to care for ourselves first and foremost, we are not able to truly serve others. It is similar to the oxygen mask guidelines given to us on airplanes: "In case of emergency, place the oxygen mask on yourself first before assisting others." If we can't breathe, how can we sustain the breath of others?

The amazing coach, Michelle Bauman, put it this way: imagine you are a teacup resting on a saucer. When you serve others from your teacup, you will drain it (you) and be empty and burnt out and have nothing left to offer yourself, let alone others. But when you serve others from the overflow of tea in the saucer, you will never run out!

When operating from the caregiver stance you want to make sure you are already full and at your optimal level before taking care of and nurturing all others in your life. When you give, give, and give some more, you will quickly become drained and worn-out, at which point resentment will build up and cause tension.

Molly was beginning to cave under her feelings of guilt and doubt, which dropped her into the lowest level of energy—her victim mode. The most draining place to be. She was exacerbating her suffering with the stories she was telling herself about what she *should* be able to do.

"What do you think your kids are saying about you when you are working until 6 p.m. and not able to pick them up every day like other moms do?" I asked her.

Her shoulders slumped slightly. "I worry that they think I don't care about them, that I'm abandoning them."

"OK..." I said, softening my voice to match hers. "Let's question that belief to see how true it is... So your kids think you don't care about them because you don't pick them up from school?" I let the room breathe for a moment. "Is that really true?"

"Well, I don't know for sure, but that's what I believe!" *Now we were getting somewhere,* I thought. The fear is in the belief she has, it is in what she imagines her children are thinking about her. And here's the truth: fear is only in our heads. It's made-up. It's not real, even if we believe it to be. It's a dysfunction of our minds. Fear and worry are misuses of the imagination, as they say.

Molly and I continued questioning her beliefs. I asked her how she treats herself and others when she believes that her kids think she doesn't care about them because she doesn't pick them up from school.

"I feel guilty: like a bad mom. And this guilt distracts me at work, making me feel like I'm not giving it my all. Then, at home, I get short with my husband and take out my frustration on him, accusing him of never doing anything to help with the kids. To stop feeling bad about not being home as much, and to make up for my absence, I buy stuff for my kids. And none of this really works. I still end up feeling guilty. I feel helpless."

"All right," I said, putting a little gusto in my voice, hoping to nudge her from this disempowered state and into a state of ownership. "Let's talk about how you would be if you *never* had the belief that your kids thought you didn't care about them... Imagine walking into the house and seeing your kids when you got home from work. How would that feel *without* the guilt of not having picked them up from school...? How would that moment feel for you if you believed they never felt abandoned?"

"Well," she said, "I would be excited to see them. I would feel energized and ready to play a game with them. I would be relaxed, and I would laugh and have fun with them." Her imagination was carrying her to a much more desirable reality.

"Fantastic! Look at the difference a thought can make in how we can feel and act. Think about what happens when you believe the thought: you treat your husband poorly, you're distracted at work and perhaps make mistakes. And you're exhausted from guilt and stress when you get home. Compare that to what happens when you don't believe that thought. You come home excited, energized, and ready to play. You have fun with your kids and you treat your husband with love and respect. What an incredible option!"

She was clearly excited about the possibility of this new scenario. There was a little pink in her cheeks, as she thought about how great it would feel to be present with her children and family in that way. She was able to see an alternate reality to the one she was currently in, one that she could easily choose to live in—right now! All she had to do was entertain a different thought—a truer thought, an empowering thought—rather than giving power to an untrue belief about her children.

When she relaxed, and looked at her beliefs, she was able to clear her head and take steps toward living the kind of life she wanted. A life without these fearful thoughts holding her back. Then she came home ready to play! When she released this fear by seeing it for what it was—a misuse of the imagination—she enabled herself to show up for her kids in the way that she really wanted to.

Chapter 12

Here's the Truth...

Certain types of stress are created not by our environment or the events in it.

Let me repeat this: Certain types of stress are not created by the events in the world around us. Just try that idea on for a minute. Let it sink in.

If we eat too little, or hardly workout, or sleep poorly, we can put certain types of stress on our bodies. But mental stress, the stress created by the demands of your job or that family member you've always fought with or the troubles of your past, is the type of stress actually created by our minds. Not the events. Yep. Stress can be created by your beliefs and your thoughts; it can be created by the way you interpret the events of life.

For instance, let's say that you are let go from your position at your most recent company. You have no work lined up, and you have those mortgage payments to take care of. Food, electric, car, etc.—you have to make ends meet. And you don't know how you will do that immediately. Sounds stressful, right? Well, for some people, when they are let go from their job, they feel a sense of freedom or relief. They trust that they will find more work and take care of all their immediate needs while they go through a much-needed transition. The situation in and of itself (a person leaving a company) is neutral (neither stressful nor relieving) but the way someone thinks about the situation creates the feelings associated with it.

Even though it can be a hard concept for some people to instantly adopt, the idea that each of us uniquely gives meaning to the world we see puts us all back into a state of ownership. When we recognize that we create and assign meaning, we can then question whether that perception is disempowering or limiting.

Asking some simple questions can get a really stuck belief to budge. Try asking, "How true is this belief really? Is it actually 100% true? Is it true all the time?" Taking a moment to reflect on a belief, especially if it has been operating unconsciously in the background for years, can really loosen its grip and ease its influence. Slowing down to see this thought, and then making a choice to not instinctively act on it can pull you from the limiting cycle it creates.

Here are some other questions I find myself asking my clients or repeating silently to myself during moments of struggle. "How is this belief working for me? Is it helping me create a meaningful, rich, happy life? Is it helping me relate to others in kind and supportive ways? Is it building me up or tearing me down?" Just because something happened in the past, does it mean it's guaranteed to happen again?" As I pause and question a hidden or obvious belief, it gives time for a new light to shine into my train of thought. It allows space for new ideas to enter. And this practice alone brings massive changes to anyone willing to engage. I credit Byron Katie here for helping me discover these practices. In fact, I want to just give her a shout out: she has been an incredible inspiration to me, and she has deeply impacted my ability to help myself and my clients live without judgment (www.thework.com).

Oh, and one last note, when using this practice, I strongly recommend actually putting the whole thing down on paper. That way, you can get it out of your head, and see it with some distance, even if that distance is just the 12 inches from your face to the page sitting your tabletop. The brain, it seems, is able to process ideas differently when the ideas move from the mind to the unmoving objectivity of a written form. Slippery concepts that otherwise swirl around can shift into solid form when in black and white. Things that seemed permanent and hidden then become clear and passing in the light of day.

Chapter 13

What Story Are You Telling Yourself?
(Most of What You Believe Just Isn't Real)

You may not have a degree in creative writing or a novel you're privately whittling into shape, but most likely, you're an amazing storyteller. If you're like most people in the world, you spend all day constructing vast and encompassing stories about the world, others, and, most importantly, yourself. These aren't exactly medieval tales of triumph and loss or Greek epics like Homer's *Iliad*, but, if you're alive and walking around, it's likely that your stories are often severed from reality, posing as truth.

Their guise is subtle and convincing. You may not recognize them as stories because you've probably told them to yourself before. The evidence you have saved up to prove these points only make them more convincing. You often welcome them because you may even gain some benefit from weaving that narrative.

A story, simply, is your interpretation of a situation or a person or an event. It is a belief about what happened or what something means. It's like when you go to a movie with your friend and you both come out at the end with totally different interpretations of what happened. You have two completely different opinions of what you saw. You both saw the same exact objective thing, but the story you're telling yourself is not just what you saw but what it meant to you and what message you took from it. All that meaning is constructed in your head. Our interactions with others in our daily lives are just the same.

It's what you are telling yourself is going on in a given circumstance. It's the thought in your head that says, "I'm seeing this happen and this is what it means." At best stories can inspire us, and at worst, stories limit us in profound and lasting ways. They can create stress, discord, pain, jealousy, self-doubt, anger, resentment, self-loathing, fear, judgment, vengeance and disharmony inside us. A story can deeply block our energy flow, leaving us in the lower energy levels, functioning below our ideal threshold and remaining in a disempowered state.

Let's say you know you have a sales goal and you're working toward reaching it, but it's not happening...Maybe you start to come up with some reasons why it's not happening. You start interpreting reality based on the information you have at hand (information which is often limited). In this way, you start to tell yourself a story. You create a story to help you understanding why you're not achieving this goal, but that story is not reality, though it often feels like it is.

Maybe you say, "Well, yeah, if I were able to offer a lower price, I would be able to hit my goal. If I had a bigger travel and entertainment budget, I would be able to hit my goal. If my customers would call me back, I would be able to hit my goal. If I were more confident or smart, if my parents weren't bad to me or my husband were kinder or my job wasn't so stressful, or..."

This type of narration clearly leads to greater victimhood and frustration. Look how bad the world seems when someone believes these false stories. Look how out of control they are. How helpless. Look at all the obstacles they have to overcome in order to just make a sale. It isn't a pretty depiction, that's for sure. It's an exhausting line of thinking.

But here's the amazing part. When you question your disempowering stories (and the thoughts that support them), you change your world! It's that easy. You can reinvent your reality in a moment. In one slowed-down act of ownership.

Chapter 14

Broken Compass

Buying into limiting beliefs is like using a broken compass to navigate the Atlantic. It doesn't show us where we want to go. Worse, limiting beliefs (which are essentially beliefs that keep us underperforming or living in victimhood or scarcity) can cause trouble, leading us crashing into the reefs or the chop of a thrashing storm. Or, perhaps, they bring us in exhausting circles, until, fatigued, we roll the sails and give up.

Like me, all my clients possess some limiting beliefs. These beliefs act as roadblocks to true progress. For many, their disempowering beliefs are unconscious (and thus more difficult to overcome). From some hidden corner of the mind, these beliefs sabotage success. We mistakenly rely on these beliefs to bring us where we think we need to go, in the same way that we trust the ground to hold our feet. But instead of leading us into our ideal futures, they endanger our well-being, hinder our potential, or worse.

Imagine, for instance, trying to make more money for yourself when subconsciously you believe that wealth is harmful or that you don't deserve to live in abundance. Imagine trying to deeply trust someone when you have a firmly rooted belief that others will inevitably abandon you. These subconscious beliefs are in direct opposition to the actions you must take in order to be successful and uncover happiness. For these reasons, they have the power to keep you locked in a struggle, functioning below your highest potential.

Happiness, consequently, becomes harder to unveil.

Growing up, I had the idea that I couldn't make money teaching; that was a limiting belief. It kept me feeling at odds with myself. It kept me living a life less fulfilling than the one I wanted. The idea that money is scarce is a limiting belief. I had heard my parents say these things when I was young, and I believed them. Then I let those ideas guide me for so long. They seemed true and plain, and that was that.

So, how do we change our beliefs?

First, we slow down. Then we question the belief and gain clarity, a simple practice that we'll explore in great depth in this book. As we apply this simple process, we learn how to identify limiting beliefs and stop listening to their flawed guidance. We look up from the compass needle, and then throw the broken thing overboard. We stop reacting to these funky concepts, and start observing them for what they are.

They are not facts we can trust. They are not certain or absolute. They are made up. They are figments of our imaginations.

Somewhere in our history, we adopted them or birthed them, and so we also have the authority to disown them. To let them go. These beliefs resulted from choices we made (consciously or unconsciously) and therefore can be overwritten by new choices based on new information. And that's the good news. We can let them go, no matter where they came from.

Limiting beliefs come from a variety of sources, including well-meaning and supposed "experts" (parents, teachers, politicians, or religious figures) who teach us to believe certain things about ourselves. We trust these figures at the time, and so we adopt their beliefs. And then, we repeat these ideas to ourselves.

For instance, if you receive a less-than-stellar performance review from your boss, you can interpret this in different ways, depending on the beliefs you've adopted. You might go into the gutter with the experience, and see the situation as proof that the world is a tough, hostile and unfair place. Or, perhaps, you can see the review as an invitation to course correct. To change some of the behaviors that were suboptimal. Either way, your view of the situation could be based on the beliefs you've adopted from your parents and the ways they modeled certain attitudes. Which is common. Maybe you heard their beliefs and internalized them, repeating them to yourself so often that they gained the hardened shell of a truth. You told them to yourself so often they became the foundation for your worldview.

This is what I had done with the beliefs my parents had about money and teaching! They believed that money was scarce and that teaching certainly would not your financial well-being. And these beliefs I continued to tell myself unconsciously. They were true. Just facts. And that was that.

Limiting beliefs also continue to grow in us because they are fed by pervasive societal attitudes that reappear over and over across a variety of media. Television, movies, and music, to name a few, all shape our understanding of the world and how we fit into it. They shape how we define ourselves and what we believe is true for us and about us. Who in America hasn't in some way compared herself to a character in a film, or repeated words from a song, because they resonated so deeply with what they already believed? We are inundated with so many limiting beliefs, we get conditioned to believe them, and this flood can be discouraging. We can easily feel like there is no way to *not* take in these toxic messages.

However, when we question as many of these limiting beliefs as we can, we begin to find just as many alternatives to the so-called "truth" as there are lies. And that's the exciting part! So many new options appear when we question our limiting beliefs, and then we open up to alternative views!

Chapter 15

The Greatest Fear

I think the greatest fear all humans have is the fear of being kicked out of the 'tribe.' As a result of this fear, we tend to do all sorts of things to ensure that others like us, that they approve of us so that they'll want us to stay in the tribe, the company, the friend group, the family. We want to feel the safety and sense of belonging that comes with acceptance. We want to feel loved, of course, too. And the warmth of affection. Below those gentle welcoming feelings, though, is that gut-wrenching worry that others will condemn us and cast us out.

When I worked in the corporate world, a female in male-dominated manufacturing industries, I tended to stand out from the crowd. One could see this as an advantage (which I do now), but when I was young and less secure in myself, I wanted to blend in. I wanted to be accepted. That seemed safer to me. And just to fit in, I would sacrifice my values by allowing things to happen that were not in harmony with my beliefs. I would allow things to happen that I would feel bad about later. And worse, I would sometimes subtly or unconsciously engineer these situations.

Years ago, I was at a business event in which my boss had me seated next to a high-level leader in the company. He was a VIP to the max. And some part of me was honored to have the chance to sit next to him, believing that I was near him because I was intelligent, articulate, and good at my job. Another part of me, though, knew that he was attracted to me, that he wanted me close so he could flirt.

I was not attracted to him at all, but I had become willing to put up with his advances to feel that faint sense of approval. If I was able to charm him and continue to gain his affection, then my job would be safe, and I would feel like I belonged.

Simply put, I was sacrificing my integrity and personal boundaries to feel approval.

As we ate dinner, I felt his hand resting on my leg like a cold washcloth. And I had no idea what to do. I just sat there... feeling helpless. After all, he was a leader in the company, and if I stopped him or brought attention to the situation, I could embarrass him and lose any favor I had gained. Maybe even lose my job.

Maybe I did something to mislead him a bit, I thought. *Maybe I was flirting, and that led him on. Maybe that's what all men do at that level...* My mind raced to explain the situation, so I wouldn't have to make a scene. *What happens if I call him out? Everyone here will laugh at me. I could lose my job.*

I just sat there, his hand still on my thigh.

The food I ate rested in my stomach like a rock, and I poured wine over it to soothe my anxious thoughts till I could rush out of the restaurant carried by the excuse of being really tired. Under it all, I felt humiliated and I felt like I had compromised my integrity to fit in and to please this executive. I felt out of line with my values, and upset with myself for being complicit in this. I felt guilt for flirting and guilt for not standing up for myself. What a lose-lose scenario.

Needless to say, this wasn't the only time something inappropriate happened with this particular man. By not stopping him that one time, he would feel permitted to do it again. And he wasn't the only one to cross boundaries with me while I was in my corporate career.

This story is not unique. Many people have stories like it—even men. A colleague of mine once told me a story about his female boss grabbing him inappropriately. He remained silent about it. He just let it be and then tried to forget about it immediately. He, just like me, didn't want to make a scene. He didn't want to upset his superiors and risk losing their approval. Not making a scene felt safer to him, so he just allowed that awkward and uncomfortable situation to go on too long. And maybe some part of him, like me, also felt oddly good about getting the attention, even though it was inappropriate and uncomfortable.

Based on what I believed at the time—that I was going to be kicked out of the tribe, rejected, and disapproved of, if I stated my boundary—I allowed that situation to occur. And because I wanted approval, I even subtly created the situation. Not just once, but many times.

Now, as I've learned to slow down my fearful thinking and question the beliefs running the show, I hold myself differently in the world. I am no longer propelled by that intense fear of being kicked out of the tribe. I set simple and appropriate boundaries in a loving and firm way. That's it. No scene. No worry. Just slowing down, taking ownership, and sticking with my values.

Chapter 16

Atlas and His Burden

The world will keep spinning even when we aren't here to whirl with it. This is both a tough fact to swallow, and a very comforting one. Luckily for me, it means I'm not responsible for holding everything together. I am not Atlas nor am I burdened with his load. Neither are you. But we often believe we are, and so we loft a tremendous amount of stress onto our shoulders to bear, thinking we must carry the weight of the world.

As the stress mounts, this idea hurts us. And in the end, unintentionally of course, we hurt the ones who we are trying to help. When we're in charge of everything, holding it all together, we strip that state of ownership away from those around us. We steal from them responsibility and we create dependence. Think of it this way: when I think that I have to fix everything for someone in my life or change their feelings about something, or tie up all the loose ends trailing behind them, I end up unconsciously stripping them of their power to change these things on their own. I end up gutting them of their right and ability to make meaningful choices for themselves. How about that? My intention is to help, and I end up hurting.

It's time to abandon the Atlas Complex and see that I can indeed contribute worthwhile things to the world, while others, too, get to live their lives on their own terms. I can certainly support others, but I need to keep my ego in check and not convince myself that their world will collapse without me there to prop up the spinning globe for them.

The coaching I've received from Steve Chandler has helped me see this, and I have since helped others to see this, too. Once they do, their relationships actually flourish more deeply than the codependent model we can unconsciously establish with the people we want to support. Once we stop micromanaging the lives of those around us, we learn to support our colleagues, family, and friends in ways that empower them to make bold choices, rather than direct them in the way we think they should go. We stop worrying so much about them. Instead, we trust their innate gifts and their ability to ask for help when it's needed. By letting go of my claim on other peoples' burdens, my energy is freed from unnecessary worry about others. It becomes ready for reassignment to something more productive.

I know this from my own life. When I stop being their Atlas—and when I'm free of my codependent worry—it's easier to be in loving union with others around me. Then I can offer myself as a bonus to their lives. I get the opportunity to cherish and nurture our connection, rather than pay tribute to some grim obligatory duty to hold everything together. As I shrug off the weight of the world, I get to assist others in identifying their strengths *and* take some time to see the wonderful alignment of the stars as well.

Chapter 17

I'm Not Needed, and Isn't that Awesome?

I could barely pick my head up off the couch pillow that had been supporting it for days. I grabbed my phone, and held it weakly in my hand. I had been taken down by a strong debilitating flu for the last five days. Ugh. Every part of my body hurt. Everything took too much energy, even dialing Steve's number: the same number I had punched into my keypad a hundred times before. I was not looking forward to the coaching session, but I knew there could be some powerful shifts, so I put my achy head to the receiver, and opened my mouth.

"I have been totally unproductive and not prepared to talk through anything with you today," I said to Steve, before he could even greet me.

"Okay. Tell me about what's going on," he said in his calm, brassy voice.

"Well, Jonathon was gone these past few days, because he was attending his grandmother's funeral, so, luckily, I didn't have to worry about him or take care of him. I could just lie on the couch and rest, letting my body fight off this flu. And I feel guilty about doing that and not getting anything done for my clients in Chicago that I will be taking care of next week."

So let's go back to your comment about worrying about and taking care of Jonathon. What makes you believe that Jonathon needs you to take care of him at any time?" Steve's response was a shock to me. I thought we were talking about my guilt for not being prepared for our conversation, but he turned it around to

63

my relationship with my son right away.

"I'm his mother! Of course he needs me!" My immediate response flew from my mouth as fast as the words could come.

"Who says?" His relaxed voice stood in complete opposition to the pressure tightly-wound tension in my own. He has such a way of putting things that even when he simply hands back what you've said, he makes the words a lesson in and of themselves. His flip tone here spoke volumes.

"Everyone knows a mother is supposed to take care of her children!" I quipped. That was when Steve began bringing my unconscious beliefs to the surface light.

"OK, so given the belief that you're his mother and mothers are supposed to take care of their children, is it true that he needs you?"

"Yes!" I was still a little indignant.

"Do you know for certain that it's absolutely true he needs you in order to survive and to function properly and get through his day?"

We both paused for a moment and let the question breathe.

"Well, no. It's not absolutely true, because I guess his dad or stepmom or the sitter we have would step in if I couldn't do it."

"Yes... So what is the opposite of this belief: 'I'm the mom and my son needs me'?" He was referring to an exercise from Byron Katie, who suggests (in the exercise that we explore throughout this book) that we flip beliefs around to see if they still hold up.

"I guess the opposite would be this: 'My son doesn't need me.'"

"Yes, that's one of them," he said holding true to the fact that this idea might sting a bit, but only inasmuch as it would eventually help. "You are not his oxygen, Sher. You are not his lifeline." He paused for impact. "You are a bonus in his life! A gift!" As soon as he said that, he asked for another. "So what's another way to look at this belief, another way to flip it around? On yourself?"

This method helps break down the unmoving stagnant components of an old belief, allowing the belief to become fluid and changeable. When we see varying concepts of a single belief and understand how these can be just as true as the first one, our old beliefs start to shift.

"I need to take care of myself."

"Yes! You are sick. Your body wants to rest, to recover and get healthy again, so you can be your best for your son and your clients and all the others in your life. *You do* need your own attention."

"Wow... I get that! I guess I am so used to taking care of things in everyone else's life and controlling my surroundings, that when I can't control being sick, I feel like I'm failing. But in fact I need to be focusing on my own well-being, not on what I think everyone else needs."

"It's called hitting the pause button. Being sick is hitting the pause button on your life and letting yourself heal until you're back to optimum health. The beautiful part of being sick is that you get to pause and then create anew when you're feeling better."

"Wow... I love that! I get to start fresh! I don't have to pick up where I left off... I get to start again and create what works best for me now."

"Exactly. Don't you LOVE being sick? What a gift!" he said, laughing.

He was right. It was a gift. It allowed me to ease up on my unrealistic expectations of myself.

Steve taught me that no one in our lives actually needs us. I know this can sound like a strange lesson, but can you see the power in it? Do you see how it can help us actually connect with others without the selfishness of martyrdom that ends up draining our resources and blocking us from really helping them?

I share this lesson now with many of my clients who deal with the same issue. They come to me bursting at the seams with guilt and mired in shame for the help they aren't giving to those in their lives. They hold themselves to unrealistic standards and beliefs, thus setting themselves up to be failures at their own game. They believe they are needed to take care of their employees, their colleagues, their kids, their spouse, their parents, their friends. And they feel like a failure when they can't take care of them all. It's not even necessary.

It's a bonus—a gift—that we're in their lives. What we offer and how we help are bonuses to them! And they are bonuses to us. It's up to each one of us to be the kind of gift people love to receive, not the ones they want to return or "re-gift"!

Before this session with Steve, I was feeling overwhelmed with all the preparation I needed to do for the upcoming client sessions I had in Chicago. I had three different organizations I was coaching at the time, and I had asked them to come well-rested and fully prepared. The least I could do was show up prepared as well! Since I was sick, I was not able to work like I had wanted to, and my unconscious beliefs that I hadn't done enough stole even more energy from me. I felt shame and guilt for not being perfect—for not living up to the unrealistic expectations I'd given myself.

The day after the session with Steve, I got up the next morning and was able to knock out three client presentations and create the materials needed for them to be valuable and useful to all my clients' sessions. What's more, I did so in record time. All my previous beliefs about myself hadn't created that kind of efficiency. Allowing my sick body to rest, relaxing and holding the view that what I have to offer is a gift, all helped me complete those tasks quickly. I was so pleased, as the material flowed effortlessly. I felt great about what I was able to bring with me to Chicago. I felt like a bonus. And all that came from shifting a deeply held, long-standing belief that just, in plain words, didn't serve. Isn't that funny that my thoughts about people needing me actually didn't serve them at all? When they don't need me, I can indeed make a more useful impact on their lives.

Chapter 18

Mother's Guilt

Cindy was a mom of two girls in middle school and had recently become a partner at a law firm when we began our coaching. Her work was demanding, yet she found it extremely rewarding. She loved what she did and had worked very hard to become the success she was.

That said, she spent much of her time languishing in her self-imposed guilt. While she believed that her girls needed her at home more often, she also wanted to be "all in" at work. She loved her family time and being a part of the lives of her daughters and husband, *and* she wanted to continue progressing in her career.

This conflict between work and family was shrouded in her desire to serve, to serve both her daughters and her clients. Underneath this desire, though, was a concern that her daughters could not get along without her constant attention, that her children really *needed* her. And this is where the guilt lies—in her belief that her daughters actually truly need her constant attention and that she will be failing them and her duty as a mother if she is not there *all the time* to take care of them. So when the job requires her attention, she feels like she is not fulfilling her role as an "ideal mother."

Once we slowed down and dug in to expose the root of her beliefs, she was able to take ownership of her experience. She could determine steps that would lead toward a more meaningful and empowering relationship with her daughters.

Our session went something like this:

"I am a bit distracted today because my daughter is at her first overnight camp and I was not able to see her off," Cindy started with.

"So what got in the way of seeing her off?"

"Well," she responded. "I have this big trial taking place at work right now, so I was needed there."

"Wow... I bet your client was thrilled to have you there," I said. "How often does that opportunity come along? Trials are not every day in your business, are they?"

"No, actually it's a pretty big deal, and I worked so hard preparing. I knew we had a good position and that I could help the case go favorably by being there."

A flash of enthusiasm rose in her voice, but her face was still knotted in conflict, the outward suggestion of her inward guilt.

"You love being a mom, don't you?" I asked.

"Yes, it's an amazing privilege."

"I completely agree. And when you believe your kids' happiness depends on you being around all the time, it can create a sense of conflict when you can't, right? In that you want to be in two places at once—- by their sides and at your job."

"That's right. I can feel so stuck sometimes," Cindy said.

"If you slow down, though, and ask yourself some questions in that moment of feeling stuck, you will be able to identify what options you truly have and then choose one. This might free you up from that stuck feeling. You might find that you prefer to be with your children at a given point or you might find that you prefer to be elsewhere: at work, or with a client. But you have the power to make these choices on an individual basis."

"Okay. So, how does that work? What questions do I ask myself?"

"If you're willing," I said, "let's play with these two scenarios you have."

"I'm game!"

"So let's start with your daughter going to overnight camp and you believing the thought that she needs you to send her off. What's going on for you internally when you believe that thought?" I asked, reminding her that we have the power to choose to believe thoughts or not. Thoughts only have emotional consequences when we buy into them.

"I feel guilty that I have to be at court with my client and can't be with my daughter at her first overnight camp send off."

"Help me understand the idea that you are "sending her off." What does that mean? Are you with her as she's in the parking lot ready to board the bus?"

"Yes. And I have to be sure to check to make sure she has everything. And I have to comfort her if she is nervous."

"By standing next to her (assuming she is standing next to you as she may want to be with her friends instead), you believe that helps her be less nervous. Is that right?" I asked.

"Yes. Typically I am the one that helps her with homework, gets her to dance practice on time (her instructor is not patient), takes her to the doctor, etc. Whenever she gets stressed, I'm there to support her," she responds with earnestness.

"When you believe the thought that she needs you when she feels nervous, but you are required to be somewhere else for work, what happens?"

"I feel helpless that I can't be in two places at one time. I feel like I'm letting my daughter down by choosing work over her. I know I don't have a choice in the matter; I have to be at work. But I feel stuck between these two places—my daughter's side and my client's side. One part of me wants to be at work, but I feel horrible that I can't be with my daughter to take care of her."

"OK, now we're getting somewhere! So, being with a client in court, you feel that you didn't actually have a choice? How true is that?" I was trying to help her find her power and take ownership for the situation.

"Well, when you put it that way, I guess it's not true that I didn't have a choice. I got into this business knowing this is how it works, and I love the times we get to be in court as everything comes together in those moments."

"Great! So let's go back to your allegedly nervous daughter who needs you coincidentally at the same time your client does. Has your daughter told you specifically that she's nervous about the camp? Has she said anything or done anything specifically to demonstrate this to you?"

"Well, she didn't say anything specific, I just know... I'm her mother. And I know."

"Ahhh, interesting. So do you actually know? Or are you guessing? Are you making an assumption without asking her what's really going on?" She was nodding slightly. "In other words, because you're her mother, you get to decide how she's feeling. It sounds more like an expectation you have that she *should* be nervous because this is her first time away like this. It makes sense you would assume that she feels that way. It also makes sense that you feel like you don't have a choice but to miss the 'send-off' and be in court with your client because your client needs you, too." I paused for a moment. "What options do you have to help your daughter with any potential fear she has about going to the camp?"

"Well, I guess I could ask her how she's feeling and what might help her feel good about the upcoming experience."

"Great! What else can you do?"

"I can talk to my husband and see if he is able to take the time off to be with her for the send-off since I will be unavailable."

"I love it! What else?"

"I can talk to one of her friends' moms and ask if she can be with her to help her with any fear she may have. I really do want to be with my client in court. The case's outcome depends on my testimony, and I've worked hard to get ready for the trial. I know we'll do a great job."

"Fantastic! What else can you do for your daughter that would let her know you are excited for her and have confidence in her ability to handle any challenge that comes along with this new experience at camp?" She was getting as excited about the possibility of empowering her daughter, as she was about seeing her daughter flourish as a confident young woman.

"I can call her or text her to see how it's going and be there for her when she comes back to tell me all about it!"

"Beautiful! Now, we can do the same thing for the belief you have that your client needs you in court," I said, encouraging her to see that her client, too, may not *need* her in the way she imagines.

"No, that's OK. I get the point! I am excited to choose being in court for my client, and I can see that my daughter is just fine and will have a new experience that we can talk about when she's back," Cindy concluded.

Working with Cindy really resonated with me, because Cindy's experience with her daughter is a common dilemma I have had many times with my own son. It was cathartic to help her see a more empowering relationship with her daughter, in the same way I've done in my own life.

Like Cindy, I create stories about what's going on in my son's mind without asking him directly how he feels. This is unfair to him, of course. And to me. It puts too much undue stress on me and takes power away from him.

Cindy's experience also demonstrates that we always have more options than we think. When we slow down to analyze our beliefs and to identify what's fueling them, we loosen our controlling grip on *their* world. When we let others make choices for themselves without believing they "need" us to always carry them through life's challenges, we are liberated from the responsibility of other peoples' happiness and security! It truly is amazing how freeing it is to let go of the thoughts that others need us. As my coach Steve said, we are in their lives as a bonus and a gift! Not to micromanage and insulate them from all of life's bumpy (or beautiful) experiences. Our roles in the world are not to be stuck in victimhood with those that need us, but to be creative beings, each and every one of us, responsible for the wonderful things we get to create in our own lives.

III.

MASCULINE AND FEMININE ENERGY

Chapter 19

In the Boys Club

"There are four things a woman needs to know. She
needs to know how to look like a girl, act like a lady,
think like a man, and work like a dog."

~ Caroline K. Simon ~

Fluidity is key. Being able to use different skillsets is
essential to the slowed-down successful life. When
people think they are stuck with only one tool, they
become rigid and stressed. Problems become harder to
solve. "When the only tool you have is a hammer,
everything looks like a nail," as they say. And this isn't
a recipe for success.

For many of my clients, sometimes they are needed
to lead the team, take aggressive action, and be forward
in their social attitudes. Other times, they will need to
listen, tap into their intuition, and make time to be
creative, patient and supportive.

Many of my female clients, high performing women,
have learned to use assertive masculine traits so well
that they can rely on this skill. In fact, they have become
so accustomed to this that some have lost touch with
their feminine attributes. They become stuck and cut off
from a tremendous reservoir of their innate power.
Worse, many of them feel at odds with themselves as
they hide the female energy that naturally resides within
them.

On the flip side, it's bad for them when they are limited to just feminine traits. In this way, they abandon many skills that are also available to them, many skills that can help in the corporate environment, such as collaboration, diplomacy, and inspiring others creatively. Women who can effectively tap into both masculine and feminine energy traits are actually better off than anyone that has just one skill set, no matter how well developed it is.

By working with my clients and fine-tuning my own energies, I have found that there is an ideal balance for naturally feminine women. Women who have feminine traits feel best when they engage their feminine side 60% of the time, and allow the masculine 40% of the time. This ratio provides a chance to be in flow with the self, while adjusting to the moment and accomplishing what needs to get done. This balance facilitates the most productive behaviors, or at least that's what my experience says.

And, just to note, my observations are based on the very unofficial research I've conducted over the last 30 years of my adult life. I have not studied these concepts in an academic environment, but the field research of the corporate world has truly demonstrated the concepts again and again. I have my own experiences and those of my clients.

Here's the problem for many of my clients. To fit into a male-dominated corporate culture, they think they have to be one of the boys. When they do so, it's like wearing a clunky lead suit. It inhibits the self, constricts movement and intuition. In it, everything takes more energy and effort. They stifle themselves in this performance, even though the traits that come with the masculine energy can help them succeed in the corporate world.

In my experience, when women force themselves

into a mostly masculine world and lose touch with their feminine energy, they take on certain traits that can be hard to deal with, traits that are exhausting for them and others. They become domineering, over-thinking, too busy, cold, blocked, overly analytical. They lose touch with their authentic, natural, compassionate, flowing, intuitive, calm, nurturing, creative whole-brain thinking.

My clients notice this happening to them, and they come to me crushed, at times, with stress. They are worn out and tired. Suffering. They feel like something fundamental is "off." I completely understand these experiences, having been that way for many years in my corporate roles. I got too caught up in my success and a desire to fit in with the boys. My ability to do so benefited me in terms of career status, but it kept me feeling tangled up in actions that denied me the kinder, gentler, softer side I felt I always had. And this practice swept from me a sense of well-being.

I have a great exercise you can do to determine if you're out of balance or not. I call it a mini-360. Take a sheet of paper and write down a list of words that you would use to describe yourself. List the traits and characteristics that you believe others would use to describe you. Now, make a phone call to one person at work—it could be your boss, a colleague, a customer, or a direct report. Tell them you are doing a quick exercise and want to ask them to give you a few words that they would use to describe you.

That's it. Don't give them any hints. Don't elaborate. Just ask them for a few traits or characteristics that best describe you. Next, compare the lists. Yours and theirs. How similar are they? Where do they differ? Reflect on where they differ and how you would like to adjust your engagement with them going forward to be more aligned with who you want to be, i.e., the qualities you wrote on your list. This isn't a foolproof technique—the people who you ask can be as unaware or single-minded as we can—but the exercise is a great place to start. A great way to gain some perspective.

When I did that exercise (the mini-360), and then reflected back on the differences, I discovered that, too often, I had a tendency to jump in and take care of things because I thought it would be easier for me to do it and get it done the way I wanted it to be done. I found myself jumping in and "rescuing" coworkers who may have been struggling to get a task done on time. With my caregiving nature, I assumed I was helping them. I had an underlying belief that they weren't capable of doing things "right," just like my husband was not capable of doing many things "right" at home. And the obvious solution was for me to step in. You can easily see how this leads to burnout, conflict, and stress for all those involved. I would create storms, not calms.

My domineering, controlling pattern of behavior was based on a judgment that others would not succeed without my help, or would do so inefficiently. While I truly thought I was "helping," I was, in reality, insulting them, stifling their development and fostering co-dependency. By relating to others in this way, by "helping," I felt like I was *needed*, important, and validated. Honestly, these feelings were just what I was looking for. But striving to fulfill these feelings in this way actually accomplished the opposite of what I wanted. "Helping" to feel needed and validated actually drove people away from me and created greater tension, not harmony and union.

What I've come to discover is that true leadership is inspiring others to step into their brilliance. Allowing them to test their skills and capabilities, without needing to swoop in all the time. To let them learn and continue to expand their skills while becoming more independent and productive in their roles.

Chapter 20

The Inner Dance

To quote Einstein, "Energy cannot be created or destroyed, it can only be changed from one form to another." In any given interaction, there is the possibility to shift energy. A hyper-masculine woman can shift into her feminine, and a hyper-feminine man can shift into his masculine. These two can actually help each other do so. All it takes is slowing down to make simple decisions in each moment. It merely takes looking at the present situation and asking, what is the most natural way to respond in this moment? What solutions come to me intuitively? Sometimes you will find a strong masculine response is appropriate, and other times a strong feminine one will be most suitable.

The chart on the following page is a valuable resource to remind you of the behaviors that result from balanced feminine energy and balanced masculine energy. The upper half of the chart depicts the two energies when they are ideally used. The lower half of the chart shows the pitfalls of swinging too far to all feminine or all masculine.

The Masculine Feminine Polarity at Work

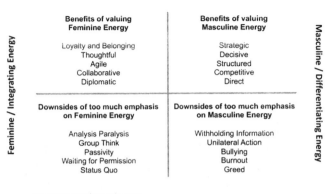

Source: www.goodmenproject.com

Source: www.goodmenproject.com

Some people who are stuck in too much masculine energy can become bullies, whether male or female. This was the case for me. Some become too stressed to think straight. Me, again. Many cause suffering in their relationships as a result of this. I personally lived for many years out of alignment. My masculine energy was dominant for over 25 years, and I felt it. In hindsight, I can see just how much this made me struggle. I loved being in the manufacturing environment. However, I often turned into a bully just so I could be "heard". I also burned the candle at both ends, because I believed that I had to work hard and play hard to keep up with my male colleagues.

I can't recall having many all-feminine energy moments. But I did know many men and women who fell into "analysis-paralysis" and "group think" tendencies that come with too much feminine energy. Being thoughtful and building consensus is one thing, and never making decisions is another. I remember meetings that became mired in these pitfalls. I remember watching the clock tick so slowly, hour after hour, minute after minute without a decision being made, grinding my teeth, feeling helpless and frustrated, while the bully in me was boiling and judging and planning a takeover.

Knowing now the impact of imbalanced masculine and feminine energy, I wish I had learned how to deal with these sooner. I would have been a stronger leader, set appropriate boundaries, honored my time, been accountable for timely decisions and actions, and been more aligned with my inner wisdom allowing creative solutions to flow more freely. I would have also practiced more patience with my teams' anxieties, while still helping to lead them efficiently and powerfully to our goals and results.

I could have increased my awareness by slowing down, getting curious, asking empowering and clarifying questions to shift into collaboration with others. Instead, I was stuck in the bottom right-hand corner of the polarity chart. I could have co-created healthy agreements, rather than taking unilateral action and barreling over people. In fact, doing these things would have been more aligned with my true nature, however covered and obscured it had become by the overly masculine bully I could be.

If you find yourself burned out and exhausted from living in your masculine energy most of the day, try putting a few of these into practice.

- Listen to flowing, soft, feminine music.
- Take a walk in nature (it doesn't have to be a long walk, just be sure to actually get out there and fill your lungs with fresh air).

- Take a bath and light candles… Be luxurious and enjoy the sensuous experience of warm water and fragrant soaps.
- Paint, read, plant some flowers, sing, play an instrument, write. Be creative!

Whenever you find yourself with a colleague stuck in too much feminine energy, you can help them get equal access to its opposite. When you see people overthinking, stuck in analysis-paralysis, and unable to make decisions, you can ask them a series of questions to get back into balance, and then move ahead.

- What is the next step for you to take in order to meet the deadline?
- Who wants to get the discussion started on this topic for today?
- What can you do about that?
- What will your turnaround time be?
- What format will the information be in?
- Who else are you depending on to complete this?
- When will I get an update on your progress?

The purpose of these questions is to get out of inaction! Move forward, be flexible, collaborate, and take action.

I like to think about all this with a metaphor. I picture the balancing act of masculine and feminine energy swaying across the dance floor. At times, you may have your feminine side take the lead, and direct the dance for awhile. Then, perhaps, the masculine side is needed, and this polarity will guide the movements. The important thing here is to slow down into the situation, stay flexible, stay aware, and stay attuned to yourself, your organic tendencies *and* the situation at hand. In this way, the whole of your day can become a more joyful, fluid, dynamic swing through each moment and whatever is needed.

Chapter 21

Masculine and Feminine in My Life

I was attending a retreat in Chicago when the facilitator drew two columns on the board, and began adding words. Above the left column, she wrote 'Masculine Energy.' On the right hand side, she wrote 'Feminine Energy.' I sat in my seat, eyes riveted to the board, as she created a distinction that put so much of my life into perspective.

She wrote:

Masculine Energy	vs	Feminine Energy
doing	vs	being
analytical	vs	intuitive
concrete	vs	abstract
striving	vs	tranquil
directing	vs	nurturing
assertive	vs	receptive
left brain	vs	right brain
organization	vs	synthesis
logical	vs	creative
busy	vs	calm
hard	vs	soft
controlling	vs	allowing

Let me explain how these ideas helped me better understand my life. I spent so much of my life utilizing my masculine energy. It helped me tremendously—to succeed, to achieve, and to get desired outcomes. It also eroded my relationships and strained some of those I really loved. At times, I became controlling, and so stubbornly committed to my own success that other areas of my life suffered. By mostly leaning into my masculine energy, I put myself at odds with what I now see as my authentic nature—a balance, with my feminine energy in the lead.

Back then, I smothered this aspect. I excluded it from much of my life. In doing so, I severed myself from a tremendous source of creative power. With access to my feminine energy, my success now is much more authentic, natural, and sustainable. Personally and professionally!

I spent most of my corporate career in male-dominated industries. Since I was one of a few female engineers in college, I was accustomed to that kind of environment. I liked it. I felt at home there. I had been developing masculine traits since high school. To me, those qualities were associated with success. If anything, I was extremely ambitious. While I smothered my feminine side, my masculine side flourished. The leadership teams were mostly male, so when I started in the manufacturing domain, I fit right in, or so I thought.

I can see these tendencies all throughout my romantic life, too. I can see the trouble this caused, as I became too controlling, too one-sided, and too assertive. It was my way or the highway, and it eroded my marriage. We were out of balance, and the natural attraction between masculine and feminine slowly dissolved under the strain.

It was truly an unfair situation for my husband at the time.

And, actually, it was a lose-lose situation! I dominated with my masculine energy, and consequently lost my attraction to him. I had resentment building, I felt like the weight of the world was on my shoulders to take care of everything, I felt the need to control things outside of me. And in hindsight, I felt disconnected and "off." For this, I blamed him partly. But I never allowed him to do anything about it. I showed up in control, domineering, taking action which allowed him to sit back, relax, go play golf, etc. Without realizing my actions were pushing him there for a release, I resented the amount of time he spent on the golf course.

At that time, I didn't know any other way.

Everything began to change in me when my son was put into my arms by his birth mother. When he was born, I finally knew what my feminine, nurturing, loving side was all about! I knew what it was like to be overwhelmingly present. What it was like to be soft and really support another. My love for my son broke through my assertive drive to succeed. It slowed me down. I began learning to appreciate simple things in life. We had au pairs from Germany come help with him, and it was a beautiful time full of connection and growth. I still wanted to provide for my family, and I enjoyed many aspects of my work, but I began to see other ways to spend quality time together and create many incredible memories! His presence opened me to a way of being I hadn't yet fully experienced.

Now, years later, and with the new understanding that I have about myself and my ways of being, I have learned to create space for my feminine energy to breathe and flourish. I have developed practices to live a fuller life. As a single mom, it's easy to let the action-oriented masculine kick in and take over. When that happens, I have learned how to balance this by also nurturing my feminine side. I take hot baths, light candles, listen to feminine music, go for walks in nature, and I even grow my hair long! These simple things connect me with my feminine energy and help me feel balanced and whole again.

Don't get me wrong... I love my masculine energy... it makes things happen and gets things done! The on-going goal for me now is to slow dance to the rhythm of both allowing each to take the lead when appropriate!

IV.

COACHING THE SLOWED-DOWN LIFE

Chapter 22

Game Film

My whole life has been a series of experiments. Until recently, I didn't know this. But there it is—my entire life. Throughout my life, I have had no blueprint to follow. No one wrote down a master agenda for me, a day-by-day, month-by-month, step-by-step plan. I had been living my life as it happened, trying out different options when they presented themselves to me. It was like an adventure. I just hadn't considered it that way before.

Upon reflection, when I realized this, it caught me by surprise. I had always thought of myself as risk-averse. Conservative. Cautious. What my friend and master coach, Melissa Ford, would call a "toe-dipper." I saw myself as that person who would come up to the edge of any given situation and put a toe in to test the water, and then act according to the temperature. Sometimes I would wade up to my waist, then run away, or, perhaps, just dangle my legs in, safely seated on the edge, in the zone of non-commitment. In my mind, I was like the person who would get close and then back off immediately after a short, two-second exposure to the chilly water.

While building my business, though, I realized that I was actually a "risk taker." And it felt pretty good to accept that title. When I reflect back on my career and how I ended up where I am today, I can see that whenever I changed direction or ventured into unknown territory, I would take the scientist's mind with me. Each decision I faced was a chance for me to experiment and test, to find out what I wanted in this new environment. Each option would be part of the formula I'd need to get a result I couldn't foresee precisely.

I studied Engineering in college without knowing where it would take me or how I would apply that knowledge in the "real world." That degree was an experiment. When I got to the "real world", my engineering degree didn't help me much. My first real job, too, was also an experiment. I never planned to work at ETC, a manufacturing firm, prior to showing up that first day. It was not on a short list of feasible options for me. My father had found the position for me while he was having a beer at the 19th hole on his favorite golf course. And I was willing to try out the job. What is that if not a willingness (and a desire) to take a risk? To think, that's how I started my remarkable career! Through sheer coincidence!

I can summarize this guiding principle of experimentation in my life in a sentence. I would take an action that would lead me to some experience, however small or obvious or dramatic the risk seemed in the moment, and each action was an experiment to see what it would produce. This attitude led me to Charleston, South Carolina, to a 20-year career at Bosch, to Germany, and back again to the U.S. to Michigan, where I've lived for 20 years.

As I look back now, I can see that no matter the result of the experiment, not a single test failed. Perhaps the outcome wasn't always immediately favorable, like the time I was laid off and wound up a single, unemployed mother in Detroit, Michigan. But if I hadn't been willing to take this approach to life, I would not have all the amazing things I have now, like my incredible son, my dream job, amazing clients, wonderful friends, my life-changing coach, and this very book.

It's no coincidence that I use this testing principle daily, whenever I am on the verge of trying something new or taking the next step in my business. When I catch myself getting anxious about making a choice, or worried that I might not like something I'm choosing to do, I slow down and remember all the experiments I've done that have gotten me where I am. I pause, breathe, and reassess. Then I shift into a higher, more inspiring level of energy. I become open to all the possibilities that this choice might birth. I trust my inner wisdom and intuition in that moment. In doing this, I get to create each day, resting in the assurance that only I am responsible for what unfolds, and that what unfolds always works, whether the outcome was planned or not.

When a plan fails to produce a desired outcome, I sometimes fall into the old habit of blaming others. Then my mind can become filled with self-pity and victim thoughts. My coach and my regular practices help me to understand when I am descending into this disempowering pattern of thought. These days, I occupy that mode of thinking for a short period of time only. I regroup and play game film, the way professional athletes do.

What is *game film*? Let me explain. I play game film when I reimagine the events that led up to my current situation, the one that has me feeling angry, helpless, or desiring to blame others. I go back through the thoughts, actions, beliefs, ideas, interactions, discussions, talks, feelings, and insights that all led me to where I am now. This activity is like going back through the lab notes, seeing exactly what steps I took, and how they led me to the outcome.

I literally replay the whole series of events in my mind or with a coach. I slow it down and take an objective look, just like a football team would do on

Monday morning when they meet for practice. They look at the films from the game before, analyzing their plays. Every pass, every fumble, and every missed opportunity for a field goal. They assess what they could do differently next time to attain a better result from a specific play. They put all these lessons into practice all week. That way they get a different outcome in the next game!

I do the same with situations in my life, and I ask myself: what can I learn from this? How can I apply what I've learned? And where do I go now?

When I play *game film* I am given the chance to assess where the agreements I made with others were not strong enough, where my beliefs were not serving me, where my actions led me off the path, and what obstacles appeared that stopped my progress. How awesome is that?

Whenever I feel that nag of failure or the sting of regret, I can turn my thoughts around to the lesson. And, if necessary, I can create a better, stronger, healthier agreement with others or myself that will yield more positive results in the future! After all, each experiment has been a success. Each has led me to this wonderful moment I have right now. Each will lead me to the next.

Chapter 23

Nothing is Forever

One of the most valuable insights my coaches have given me can be summed up in three words: Nothing is forever.

For many, permanence can be a burden: it can make us feel trapped in our choices, with no way out. Whether conscious or unconscious many of our views sound like this: "This job I took out of partial desperation is forever!" "This job I hate is forever!" "The trouble I have with my sister is forever!" "The financial trouble I'm in is forever!" On the other hand, impermanence is a license to live the life you want, allowing you to make changes when you see fit.

Seeing impermanence in everything allows you to change without fearing a loss of security, without feeling like your identity is attached to one title or achievement. As I relaxed into this understanding, as I let my fears evaporate—my fears about this reality of living without the permanence I had come to expect—I gained freedom. Impermanence allows me to make whatever choices I want in my life, without fearing that I'm making wrong or irrevocable decisions. Impermanence allows me to be free.

Many young women have come to me a few years out of college, frustrated and disenchanted with the 'real world.' Their first career jobs do not reflect any of the interests or skills they cultivated in college. But as new members of a dynamic workforce, they feel stuck and constricted; they think they must simply adapt to the career path they've chosen. What's the solution to this? Seeing what's true: this job, like anything else, is temporary. A different life is only one choice away.

In our sessions, I have these young women first focus on mapping out their path to fulfillment. We focus on short-term goals. Then I encourage them to redraw the map as they go, knowing they'll encounter forks in the road. This is the life of experimentation and trial. And when we stay open, both of these can lead us to success. When my clients open up and see that they are "allowed" to do that, to make choices and adjust as they go, a weight falls off their shoulders. They relax. They find what they want to create for now in life.

Likewise, as I work with more seasoned career women, they can enjoy this same weightlessness, as they also discover that anything is possible. My own career journey, that has led me to my current work, demonstrates this point. It's never too late to pursue a dream job, no matter how out of reach it seems.

When this idea sinks in without being accompanied by judgment or undermining doubt, it creates a spark of joyful energy and excitement. This energy, then, helps compel someone forward. I've seen what looks like years of frustration dissolve almost instantly when these principles are adopted. Impermanence and choice are the keys to creating any life you want. So repeat it with me: "Nothing is forever!"

Chapter 24

You Don't Have to Do This (Life) Alone:
An Ode to Coaching

Excuse the cliché, but I am otherwise at a loss for words. When I began experiencing coaching, which I have been experiencing for years now, I could put it no other way than this: I was that caterpillar stuck in the cocoon before working so intensely with my coaches to transform. And now I have turned into a butterfly: freer, happier, more active and powerful than I was ever before.

If we want to get really scientific about the whole thing, which will help obscure the cliché, caterpillars actually dissolve completely in the cocoon before reassembling into a butterfly. They become a liquid. Completely liquid in the cocoon. In essence this is like my experience with coaching. My habits and beliefs had to be broken down until they were virtually unrecognizable. From there I could rebuild into a completely different mode of living. Everything about my former operating system had to change. And when it did, I came out on the other side transformed.

That said, when I first heard the word 'transformation,' it freaked me out. I feared it would mean becoming someone I might not recognize, which felt terrifying to me. My life felt safe and familiar, even if it wasn't that satisfying. The new life—the transformed life—made me worry about change, vulnerability, adjustment—basically, everything unknown. Some of my clients, too, have this feeling when they show up for an initial conversation with me. When this is the case, my goal is to show them that transformation actually is wonderful, as it uncovers what someone truly wants in the world and the ways to get that. I also want to show my clients that they don't have to tread this path alone. They can have a guide, a mentor, a coach—their biggest fan right there alongside them, every mile of the trail.

I often ask my new clients to think of coaching this way: Athletes perform better under the guidance of an experienced coach, who watches the way they engage with their sport and gives them personalized training and techniques. What successful athlete hasn't had the steady and powerful leadership of a committed coach? A sports coach sees the blocks to success, the natural talent of the athlete, however raw, and prescribes the best methods for getting his client to the desired next level in his athletic career. The coach helps the athlete see what she cannot see on her own. Life Coaching and Leadership Coaching are exactly like this. They help people perform at their best by working alongside them as they step into new territory.

This was the case for me when I embarked on my journey with my own coach, and the training I received from him came from a perspective I never would have had if I hadn't sought this kind of guidance. Now that I have had a vast array of experiences with coaching, I know that I would have benefited from this teaching years earlier. While I was getting my footing in the corporate world, I struggled on and off to find direction, and certainly I experienced more burnout than necessary. I can be stubborn at times. To a fault, even.

Finally, after 18 years at Bosch, I had my first direct experience with great coaching. Thankfully, it wasn't too late, but certainly I could have benefited earlier on in my career. My bosses, after all, had coaches themselves, and I could see the positive impacts in the way they operated.

My first coach, John Vautier, was brought into our workplace by my boss at the time. He was a speech and presentation coach hired for a handful of us on the leadership team. John Vautier was amazing. He helped us all develop our strongest attributes and qualities as speakers. He reflected back to us the power we had but couldn't yet see, and in this way, he pushed us along to our best stage performances, which, in turn, helped us in every aspect of our careers. To this day I haven't forgotten his lessons. I sometimes wonder how many lessons I would have learned over the years had I given myself regular exposure to coaching!

These thoughts about the impact of coaching led me to study coaching, to deepen my knowledge of coaching, so that I could excel in my own career and help others to perform at their best. This was the teacher in me coming out. I just wanted to help those around me to find and realize their greatest potential, as I was realizing mine.

When I decided to study executive coaching, I discovered the Institute for Professional Excellence in Coaching (www.ipeccoaching.com) and stumbled into a goldmine. At first, I had no idea what I would learn, but so many of these teachings have led me to a greater sense of purpose, self-awareness, and personal growth— more than I could have ever imagined!

For instance, I was able to envision and create my own business. I climbed over all the hurdles my fears and doubts had placed in my way, and developed my own coaching company, which was like raising another child. The work was rich with excitement as well as struggles, and filled with moments of profound gratitude and personal fulfillment. In my past life, when I was constantly flying from city to city, rushing from hotel to hotel, and meeting to meeting in a haze of worry and stress, I never could have imagined the freedom, flexibility, and security I gained by creating my own business. Alone, and without coaching, I couldn't have done it in the same way.

After I finished my certification program, I hired my first coach, a trainer at IPEC, who helped me prepare to launch my business. She rocked my world by challenging me each week in her direct yet loving way. She prodded me to hoist myself out of the mire of resentment that I had been stuck in for years. I began to forgive many in my life I had thought wronged me, seeing them as people doing the best they could. All the victim energy I had, the stories of blame and powerlessness that I had adopted in my youth and clung to in adulthood, began to dissolve.

I began growing up, maturing, leaving these victim patterns where they belonged—in the past. For the first time, I truly understood the power of personal choice. I finally recognized my ability to have the life I wanted and the relationships that were most fulfilling. I worked with my coach, Raechel, for several years and still continue to benefit from all she helped me do to take ownership for my personal life (www.thesparklingbride.com). Her impact on my life is everlasting.

There are so many incredible coaches available to help people who are stuck in their personal and professional lives. Each one has a unique approach to coaching and the way that they interact with clients. (See the "Recommended Resources" for some coaches who I highly recommend).

When I entered the world of coaching, I had all that raw wonderful potential that everyone has, and that you have in you now. I just didn't know it yet. I suffered from the victim stories I refused to close the book on, and in short, I was that grey caterpillar inching forward to a destiny it didn't yet know. While in the cocoon, I had to alter my thinking, alter my behavior, alter my life, and adjust my attitude. Just like the caterpillar breaks down completely, I had to be willing to shift my perspective in order to shrug off the protective layers I'd been hiding beneath and find who I was at my core. And how grateful I am that I had such wonderful people supporting me as I went through that remarkable transition from victim of circumstances to owner of my own, vibrant life.

I have worked with many gifted and talented coaches, but the single largest investment I ever made in myself through coaching was the choice that reaped the greatest results. When I invested in myself, I changed completely. I mention this because I had to learn how to best use a coach. I had to learn how to *best* learn. By investing fully – this included myself, my attitudes, my beliefs, my energy, my time, my money, and my ambitions—I was able to take full advantage of my time with Steve Chandler and be a good student of his teachings. It felt like a ton of money and time to invest, but each dollar and each minute helped me show up more fully, and doing this grew my business exponentially. I was fully committed and responsible for my outcomes, which immediately, in and of itself, put me in a place of ownership like I had never had before.

While I was Steve's apprentice for that year, he helped me see my power, however latent or hidden from my view. He helped me to see that I could create whatever I wanted to in this wild world, that I could make decisions in each moment that supported my deepest visions, and that I could be an owner in my life, rather than a passive participant. Fully. And with no apologies. The people pleasing and apologetic tendencies I had learned as a young girl, and which I carried like a shield into adulthood, became obsolete. Once I dropped them for good, I propelled myself into a state of action. I didn't need to apologize for my successes or ask others if it was okay for me to succeed. Rather than shrouding my ambitions and goals with a layer of social shame, I was able to participate fully in the life I wanted.

Steve helped me to uncover my suppressed boldness, so that I could grow my business to a level I had never imagined possible. I had always been successful, but had been plagued by tinges of guilt, like I didn't deserve what I had or that I somehow lucked into it, or was an imposter and was here by some grand mistake. My angst with success was due, in part, to my overactive masculine energy as much as the critical voice in my head. Steve was instrumental in helping me question and turn around my thoughts (Byron Katie style) about my family, my clients, my son, my friends, and myself, so that I could live in the world I wanted from a place of congruence. In short, working with Steve for that year, week in and week out, was one of the most transformational experiences of my life.

Being in a cocoon can feel scary and uncomfortable, but I believe that, to risk being another cliché, I emerged from that cocoon ready to fly. To put the whole thing into two words: Coaching works. And damn well.

Chapter 25

Taking Action – The Way of Success

There is an old riddle that goes like this:

There are five frogs on a log.
Four decide to jump off.
How many frogs are left on the log?

The answer is this: All five are left.

They only *decided* to jump off; none of them actually did.

Action requires putting life into motion. Taking action requires figuring out what you want, and moving in that direction. It requires verbs. You can spend a lot of time thinking about what you want, envisioning want you want, and planning it, but nothing will happen until you start to take action, get into motion or do something, no matter how small or large, simple or involved that step is. Some of my clients—like me—end up spending too much time bound up in thinking about something, in anticipation and forecasting and determining the perfect plan, rather than moving ahead. You can have all the potential in the world or a perfectly flawless plan, and it will all mean nothing if you skip this essential ingredient. You must take action!

And here's the crazy thing about this: you can start to take action even before you have a clear vision of what you want. It's okay to not know exactly what you want at first. You can start taking action as a way to explore options.

For instance, you can go and ask somebody, "Hey will you brainstorm with me some ideas about this potential career shift I'm considering? I'm looking at transitioning out of this industry into another one. Would you be willing to chat?" Finding someone who has been down your path before, someone who you know is a great sounding board, can be a great place to start. Or, if you want, find a coach. Do some research online. Write a journal entry that describes your ideal day and how you want to spend each hour. These types of actions, of talking and brainstorming and exploring, are themselves a way to get clearer.

And little steps, whatever they may be, add up. Better yet, they take you from that stagnant and idle place of sitting and thinking and evaluating and analyzing. A place of paralysis. A place of fear or perfectionism.

Paralyzing tendencies kick in often when the monster in your head starts to speak up again. The inner critic, the gremlin, starts chirping in your ears, "Well, it's probably too dangerous to do that thing you want to do. Wait until you find the right path. You need to know more. Remember when you made a mistake the last time? Remember how painful that was? Let's not do that again!" This voice is trying to protect you, to create safety, but what it really does is hold you back. It keeps you in victim energy.

The way to shift into an owner state, out of this victimhood, into that life you want to create, is to just get started by taking one step at a time. When you start to take one step, you start to get a sense of purpose. With movement, with actual physical activity, your decisions and choices and routes start to get more clear. Plus, when you're in action, you're less focused on worry and fear and what might go wrong. Instead, you're focused on the progress you're making.

Action-mindedness trumps preoccupation with problems. In this state, your attention is focused on concentrating your resources to move in the desired direction. It's not focused on potential failure. There's no room for that. No room at the Inn. There is no time. Instead, action begets action and results, which you can use to figure out your next steps.

As you gain the initial momentum of this ownership state, you'll begin to get clarity which also allows you to start slowing down and let whatever happens next to happen next. This way you're not just like a bull plowing through a china shop. You're more methodical, resourceful, and calm, which allows space in your thinking and action. A space free from the critic. In this space, you'll be able to see what happens, assess your results, and adjust accordingly. This is the experimentation mode that always yields forward progress, whether the outcomes are exactly as planned or in need of slight adjustments.

At this calm pace, we start to be kind to ourselves and say, "I'm not going to go from 0 to 60 in 2.5 seconds, I'm just going to take a step, see what happens, decide whether I want to continue on that path. If not, I'll adjust." There's no right or wrong action step to take. The goal is strictly to get started and keep moving. There's no urgency to rush to the finish line. Simply take one step at a time. Move into what feels better and better.

When it's relaxed, committed, and forward moving, then taking action is truly a creative space in and of itself. Action provides results and a chance to continue refining these results with each additional move. There are no exceptions. Action is the way to a better life.

Chapter 26

Finding The First Step

"I'm nervous, Sher," she said in her familiar tone.

Young, high performing, talented, and mother to three kids, Natalie didn't know exactly what was next for her in her career or how to get going. She and I had discussed this point several times in our coaching sessions, but she still felt a little 'stuck.'. Chance (and the result of her hard work), though, had her set up for an opportunity that was going to help her out.

As a young leader selected by her company to represent them in an industry organization, she was getting prepared for an event in the Michigan area. There, she'd be meeting a few major CEOs in her industry, which meant opportunities to hobnob with some bigwigs that she wanted to impress.

She was nervous about attending and the fact that she didn't know what to get out of meeting these high-level executives made her anxious. Our job was to slow this whole thing down and start taking action in the form of brainstorming.

"Okay, what is one thing you would like to get out of this event, Natalie," I asked her. "What is the one thing you want to learn from the experience? Think of just one or two of the CEOs and how you'd like to connect with them..." Her worry had her in a defensive mind frame. Rather than thinking creatively or constructively, she was reactive in her thinking and worrying about "how to impress them, leave a mark and manage the whole thing perfect." Her overwhelm and perfectionism had her frozen in her tracks, thinking too big, when simple steps would suffice.

"Well, I'd really like to talk about what I've been up to and just learn from them, you know?" Natalie is an incredibly curious person. "I want to know what their careers have been like."

"Good," I responded. "What else?"

"I want to know where they started. How they progressed. What struggles they came across and how they overcame them."

"So you have just a couple questions that you want to ask," I joked. "You're exactly right, Natalie! There is so much to learn from these people. They have tremendous experience and lots of wisdom, I'm sure. Having a dialogue and a conversation with them is a great place for you to get started in figuring out what your path is from here. You don't need to tackle your whole future at once. Just get started. Build a few relationships."

"Yes. It will be great, but I'm a little concerned what they will think of me..." This kind of self-focused thinking only exacerbated her fears.

"So, what if it was okay to just ask them about their lives? To just listen and connect? What if this event was actually about building relationships rather than trying to impress or wow or amaze or secure some perfect career shift? How would that be for you?"

She thought and re-crossed her legs in the leather swivel chair.

"What if you just knew that you are amazing – which you are – and trusted that that would come through in your interaction? What if you could do so without any attachment to a specific outcome?"

She was beginning to relax into the back of the chair.

"Would it be easier and more relaxed for you if you went in curious and just asked them about their lives?

And you didn't need to do anything to impress them?"

"Yes. That sounds great!"

In our next session Natalie was bursting with excitement. She had met some of the people she was excited to meet and she really enjoyed talking to them.

"Sher, one of the CEO's asked me to come in and meet with him and his company to explore possible opportunities!" She had hardly sat down before she started speaking. "But I'm not interested in leaving where I am right now."

"That's okay," I reassured her. "You could still go meet with him just to have a nice conversation and again open up to the possibility that there could be something down the road that would be interesting. Remember this is about building relationships. And when you are ready to make a change, if that happens, then you can draw on him as a resource."

Eventually, she did just that.

Six months later she was leaving her company and joining his with a large promotion and a larger scope of responsibility. This all resulted, I can say, from taking action and the first step, while slowing the whole process down. Rather than impressing and figuring out the whole future, it was about connecting. Rather than the future, it was about the present moment. Rather than fear, it was about curiosity, opportunity, possibility, and how to get moving joyfully into those states of mind.

Chapter 27

The Paradox of Having a Goal to Have No Goal

Taking action often requires that odd and seemingly paradoxical tendency to slow down. Get momentum *and* slow down— strange, right? Well, maybe not so weird… The right actions seem to present themselves often, when we slow down to create space for creativity, and when we open our eyes to the many possibilities in each moment. When we slow down the obsessive march toward a particular outcome, it becomes clear that we need to get into motion, even without the exact target in our crosshairs.

When we're rigidly clasping onto something we want, we can easily miss the real opportunity available or perhaps the other ways to get the thing we want. Well, that was the case with a client of mine.

"I've got to network, to talk to people. I've got to get the word out and let them all know!" The only thing that matched Janice's fevered pitch was the pace at which she spoke. Her words ran together as they rushed from her mouth. Janice was starting a business and felt like she had to do everything at once. And it should have been done yesterday.

"Okay," I said, wanting her to challenge this fear-based thinking and put a more productive approach in place. "How can you just start with one step, one conversation with one person? Can you focus on their biggest need and see how that relates to what you offer in your business?"

"That seems possible," she said with half belief.

"Could you go into the situation with just the simple desire to serve and build a relationship? When you do this, when you ease off your 'need' for a certain result, you can find a way to truly help people. You will build a relationship, which could potentially lead to business down the road, depending on what they are looking for and how your service can benefit them."

She was nodding slightly, while her eyes gazed out the window, focusing on something way off in the distance.

"When you try to force something you can actually stifle it with the pressure, and you shut down your creative side, and you will not be able to see how you can actually help. You'll be bent on forcing a particular outcome, which will blind you to what your client needs at that time. The fear that there isn't enough, that your needs aren't yet met, will cause you to complicate a very simple process. By building your business through actual service, it will grow much faster than building it from pressure and fear and agitation."

I could see a crack in her beginning to open. But she hesitated. "I get the concept, but I need money NOW! How do I speed up the process?"

"Let's take a minute to see who is right in front of you that you could help. Who are you meeting with next?"

As Janice began to talk about all the people she had lined up to "pitch" her service to, I asked her to slow it down.

"Let's take one at a time. Tell me about the first one on your list that you planned to meet. What do you think is going on in their world right now? Where do you think they can use your help the most?"

She began to consider the approach of not having a generic features and benefits pitch, but rather, taking a minute to really think about the person right in front of her, first on her list. We kept diving deeper into this concept, this notion of easing up. As we brainstormed about the most impactful ways to be present in the moment with each potential customer, we came up with a crazy concept.

"Can you have fun with these conversations? Can you make these playful and enjoyable for you and your prospects? What if the calls didn't have to be hardcore sales calls or hardcore business deals? What if they are just looking for connection and a sense of who they are? What if you didn't need to convince them or manipulate the situation into some kind of outcome? What if it were easy and natural, like a conversation?"

"Yeah! I could build my business from a place of connection and service! I could really enjoy my time with potential clients."

She did just that. She slowed down, she started having a great time with her clients, and she came out of her fears and began to listen intently for what was really going on in their worlds. She stopped trying to sell. And started trying to serve more deeply, focusing on how she could be helpful in that moment. She started to focus on the present, the task at hand, the person across from her, the next step and the next small action that would help her build her business. She took action, and it was a relaxed, slowed-down action that actually brought her greater joy, more money, and a higher level of success than the forced "busyness" she had filled her day with.

Chapter 28

Paint a Picture of Your Ideal Life

After two years of being the Global Sales Leader for a British cosmetic packaging company, I was exhausted and fed up with the demands of constant travel and living out of a suitcase. Simply put, I was tired of the road. I knew I wanted to leave my job and find something that truly called to me, but I didn't know where to start looking or where I wanted to go. It was frustrating. Though there were many people I cared about in my company, and I'd had many incredible experiences, each day I felt like the walls of my office were closing in on me a bit more. The regular flights felt longer, the hour-long commute to the office was draining, and the company's vision didn't excite me the way it had in the past.

The urge to find something that truly spoke to me had taken root within me. There was no ignoring that fact. My desire for a better career fit was growing stronger by the day.

So what did I do? I used a technique that I teach many of my clients. I created my vision—a crystal clear picture of my ideal future with a job, relationships, office, and income. I got incredibly specific. In my mind, I formed the details of my day-to-day life as vividly as possible, including who would be there, what we would be doing, and where.

Here is the vision that I created:

I am walking to my office in downtown Plymouth. I have 20 clients lined up for the week ahead. Jonathon is doing great in school. I am dating a wonderful man who supports me and enjoys life with me. I am earning $500k/yr. I have written two books and I am traveling a bit, giving motivational speeches. I am playing tennis and renting a house on the beach. I am going to the Ranch with Jonathon 2x/yr. I feel alive! I feel sunshine and joy with every day. I am volunteering again and making a difference in many people's lives. I have clients seeking me out. I have an assistant to help with bookkeeping and scheduling. I am spending each afternoon with Jonathon helping him develop into a kind, loving young man. I am going to the movies with my partner, holding hands, being connected. I am happy and free!

Now keep in mind, I had no idea how I was going to do it, but that didn't matter yet. What really mattered was having a target to shoot for. All throughout my life, I had made decisions along the way and had taken action as the opportunities occurred. But I had never had a clear picture of what I wanted until I set my intentions and put them on paper.

I think of it like this—without a destination in mind, a plane will never reach its target or get its passengers where they need to go. While flying, a pilot can pass any number of welcoming landing strips, but there is only one true target. Keep in mind, though, the route to that destination is not a straight line. To get to the target destination, pilots are continuously course correcting based on wind, altitude, and other variables. The same holds true for your intention to reach your destination. Be open to your vision expanding, to twists and turns on the route, and allow yourself to course correct as the path unfolds. Create the vision, then course correct.

After I did the vision exercise and set the intention to paper, within eight months, I was living 80% of what I had written! It was almost unbelievable to see the opportunities appearing in front of me. Things that had always been there, but that I had not seen or believed were for me, suddenly came into view and became attainable. With my vision in mind, I could now see what I had always overlooked. And it was very natural for me—I would say effortless—to take the actions necessary to create the life I wanted.

Many times we imagine what we would like to do for work, where we would like to live, and whom we would like to spend most of our time with, but we fail to get a really clear image of this future existence. We fail to write it down in detail, and thus miss a chance to begin working toward this vision in a tangible way, like a project. Once an intention is moved from inside your head and onto paper, clarity begins to illuminate your path and action steps are more easily seen. So, go grab a piece of paper and pen, and don't hold back. Draw the picture of the world you want to inhabit. Then begin to take the steps necessary to creating the life you've always wanted for yourself.

Chapter 29

The Power of Intention

My son and I were on our way to Denver from Detroit for summer vacation on a Sunday morning in July, 2010. He was wearing his usual Dallas Cowboy's jersey, and recited to me that morning the most recent batch of stats he'd learned. He knows everything about every player—where they went to college, what positions they've played on various teams, what their nicknames are, and on and on... Not just the recent players, but also every NFL player since the beginning of time—he knows them all!

As our plane took flight and we continued to settle into our seats in row 6, he at the window, me in the middle seat, I noticed a young woman standing in the aisle looking at us. (Since the terrorist attacks of 9/11, no one stands in the aisle anymore so I found it odd, but she seemed kind.) As I was thinking all this, she looked at me with an expression of sudden shock across her face. "Are you Sherry?" she asked, while the blood was running to her cheeks.

"Yes, I am," I said a little confused, but smiling. "Where do I know you from?"

She leaned in toward me and told me her name, then looked at my son. She was struggling to hold back a rush of tears, and her voice cracked slightly. It had been ten years since I last saw her, ten years since she agreed to choose my husband and me at the time, to be his parents...

It was my son's birth mother!

Imagine that! On all the planes, in all the cities, on all the possible flights, in all the possible rows of seats, his birth mother was right there. As plain as day.

She had recognized us, because I had agreed to send her pictures every year until my son was 18. I sent the pictures, because I wanted to share with her how he was doing and what an incredible gift he is in the world, to give her glimpses into the amazing life she had helped create. I had set an intention when we first adopted him to make sure she knew he was thriving, that she had made a beautiful, loving choice in choosing adoption. I did not know how that intention would fully play out... I thought it would be through annual letters to the agency with pictures that were forwarded on to her. Little did I know this "chance" meeting on a plane would be the incredibly powerful version of that intention in real life.

What's even crazier than that, though, is the fact that before her last minute upgrade to first class, she would have been right next to us! The universe, it seems, was conspiring to bring us all together in that very moment, on that very day, in that very plane. She couldn't miss us, it seemed. Her intention made this so.

After we got off the plane and went to get our luggage, she was waiting for us in baggage claim to talk a bit more. She gave my son a hard time for wearing a Dallas jersey instead of a Detroit Lions jersey. As they chatted, she was able to match all the stats he threw around. Come to find out... she was a Fantasy Football champion! How crazy is that...? This football obsession must be in the genes! I certainly didn't have it, but these two paced each other perfectly.

After they exchanged boatloads of numbers and figures and names, we said goodbye, gave her a big hug and went on our way. The coincidence of the experience, though, stayed with me that entire month, then for the year. It still lingers with me now, as I write this, many years later. Her intention, whatever it was precisely, and mine were so powerful it brought us all together. She taught me such a wonderful lesson about the importance of holding our visions for our lives. Constantly.

Chapter 30

Dolls in a Row: Finding My Coaching Calling

When I was ten, I used to gather up my play chairs and set them up like a makeshift school in the basement of our house. Then I'd collect my dolls and set one upright in each seat. They'd become my well-behaved students I wanted them to be, and I'd take my place at the head of the room to teach. Some days they would learn math. Other days, English. For about two years, I gave them their regular education; the little semicircle of motionless faces listening intently to my lessons. At the front of the room, with my good little listeners in a row, I was totally in my element. I was teaching, and I loved it.

That said, for most of my life, I thought I didn't know what I wanted to be. I thought I didn't really have a calling. I felt, at times, a little lost. I was just focused on the next obvious success. I was focused on the path I unconsciously picked up from those around me. To do what I really wanted would have felt like a great risk, a stepping out of the known. When I look back, though, I can see my own interests expressing themselves in much of my life.

As I entered high school, the desire to teach grew. I tutored my younger brother at the kitchen table for hours. He struggled with dyslexia, and his Catholic school was not very supportive of his learning needs. So I stepped in to help him, to work with him closely on understanding and completing his lessons. It was no mystery to me, or to my family, that I loved this kind of work. I loved helping others see for themselves that they could do whatever they set their minds to, even if someone else had told them they couldn't. I especially liked that, proving that he could succeed.

My father, though, wanted me to study engineering, because there was no money in the classroom. As a good little girl I did what my father wanted. And then I stayed on that practical path. I put aside this teaching idea, and instead aimed for financial success. Looking back, I can see that I was not attending to my own wants. I was placing too high a priority on money. I was people pleasing and not following my deep desire. Despite all this, my longing to teach never went away. It only hibernated in me, and expressed itself in any teaching opportunities that I came across.

Twenty-two years after I enrolled in college, I was let go from my job as senior vice president of global sales at an American automotive component supplier, and I started a consulting company that helped multinational sales teams grow business for major corporations. While working on a contract with a Japanese supplier in the automotive industry, I spent much of my time teaching and coaching their sales team about how to maintain strong and healthy customer relationships while raising prices to match global economic changes, which, of course, was the sales team's worst nightmare. Not easy, but rewarding.

The ten-year-old girl inside me, who taught her dolls addition and spelling, was loving this work. I was being paid to help others grow in their professions in meaningful ways. I was teaching powerful skills, like how to interface effectively with customers from different cultural backgrounds, and I was instructing them about how to develop visions for the future, like creating inspiring strategies to expand and diversify a company's customer base. It was great.

In spite of a fulfilling year as a consultant, I fell back into believing I needed a "real job", and that doing what I loved wouldn't sustain my financial needs for long. Fortunately, I was able to join a global cosmetic packaging firm as the Global Sales Leader. This job was amazing! I went to dinners in castles in Paris, and was paid to work with customers in New York, Brazil, China and other European locations. I was working with a worldwide, multi-cultural team of amazing, talented people, who met as a team regularly to inspire one another to do their best.

These meetings were creative and empowering. Our customers loved our new global network and the high performance that resulted from this approach. Not long after we started, the company decided to sell the business. I was at a defining moment in my life: I could go back to the automotive industry, or start my own leadership consulting firm. Having again had a taste of the powerful effect teaching had on my sense of career fulfillment, there was no way I could go back to something else. Besides, my consulting stint had taught me a desperately needed lesson: There *is* money in teaching.

With this attitude, I decided to get certified in professional coaching, and off I went. Never to look back!

I learned another equally important lesson from all these experiences. I learned that anything you envision for yourself is possible. The result may simply look different than you originally planned.

When I was a child and a young woman, I imagined myself one day becoming a schoolteacher, positioned in the front of the class, dictating course material to eager students. Financially tight, of course, but doing what I loved. But after my career in the corporate world, I learned that teaching could be absolutely different than that. I could stay in the environment I had been succeeding in for years, and still be an educator.

Rather than sifting through equations on a blackboard, or pacing in front of hundreds of students in a lecture hall, I now teach people in a different way. I help people find and realize their life's vision. I get to design relevant and useful material for my clients, knowing that the more value I offer them, the more potential they have to become wealthy in all aspects of life. Naturally, the more value I offer as a coach, the more prosperous I become as well.

Chapter 31

Finding Support for My Vision

When I started my leadership coaching firm, I knew that I wanted to impact my clients deeply. I knew I wanted to make a profound difference in the world. I had the sense that I had to get some help to do this. I knew that this would require me to invest in coaches for myself, who would help me to further develop the coaching and mentoring skills I already had, and unearth new skills that could help me maximize my service to my clients.

The first step I made in this direction was to consult with a business coach. I hadn't realized that running a business is not the same as having a coaching practice. I hadn't realized that starting a coaching practice was truly akin to becoming an entrepreneur, and would take a different type of business strategy than I had experienced managing sales for a global company. I had big dreams of having an international coaching business, helping people around the world to live their most inspired lives and do the kind of work they would find most fulfilling. However, I didn't know exactly how to make this dream a reality, from an economic and entrepreneurial perspective. My coach helped launch me in the direction I needed to go, and gave me the tools I'd need to find my way successfully.

After I felt confident in what I'd accomplished with a business coach, I hired another coach to help me with relationships in my personal and family life. During our time together, this coach proved to me the many ways coaching positively impacts multiple areas of my life. I found that I could create for myself the same things I wanted to help others create! My experiences with these two coaches shaped my own coaching career and pointed me in the direction that I wanted to go as a coach and a teacher. They helped me articulate and define the most compelling version of teaching I could muster.

After working with these two coaches, my life became forever altered by my time working with the true Master Coach, Steve Chandler. When I read his book, *The Prosperous Coach*, I knew immediately that he was the one to help me truly thrive in this next phase of life. Little did I know I would invest heavily in this experience by working alongside Steve as his apprentice for a year, just a few months after reading his book! I was done dipping my toe in the water and living on the edge of doing something great. After a long career doing something I was good at, but not passionate about, I was finally ready to make my life happen exactly as I had always wanted. Coaching and teaching were to become the central forces in my life, and I would never look back from this defining moment.

Chapter 32

How I Teach Now

My desire to create my own firm, Sherry Welsh, LLC, was inspired by the transformational work that took place in my own life. It sprang from the changes I created in the way I lived and worked. I had found a happier, more productive, useful and prosperous way to live, so the obvious next step for me was to help others make this same transition. As I worked with Steve and began to truly prosper on my own, I realized that I could help others do the same. I knew it didn't mean they had to leave their jobs and start over like I did. Through my coaching, I created an environment in which high performers could get clarity, increase their focus, and slow down their rushed and inefficient thinking, so that they could thrive wherever they chose to be!

That's right: my style of coaching is all about choices and ownership. It's about empowering people to identify their own victim mentality or reactive living, turn away from it, and walk in the direction they truly desire to go. Building this environment led me to find my ideal clients, and so I began to make the life and career that I really wanted. I listened carefully to my own desires to find and serve my ideal clients as powerfully as I could. It worked. It continues to bring me together with the people I am meant to coach.

The life I'm living now is miles away from the rows of dolls I instructed for years in our musty basement. However, just as the fun of my playtime fueled my passion then, the work I do now feels uplifting and personally fulfilling. I get to help people create the most amazing lives they can imagine for themselves, and I get to have fun doing so. I had lived many years disconnected from my true calling, at odds with myself because of the decisions I'd made, and trudging dispassionately through a career that constricted me. Now I get to live as I am intended to. I get to create the exact life I want for myself, and the best part is, I get to help others do the same.

Chapter 33

Unfulfilled Achievement

Imagine putting all your effort into one thing. You have a single-minded goal and nothing can budge you from the course you've set to reach that goal. It will be yours. And when you finally achieve it, you know you will be at ease, able to rest. You will finally feel happy and content! As soon as you achieve that one thing... Satisfaction!

Now imagine that when the happy day of success comes, you don't feel relieved and accomplished. Instead, you feel frustrated. Off. Or just kind of blah... You had worked so hard and expected so much. Then, blah. This experience would be like living in some mythological Greek hell. (Tantalus comes to mind, that starving guy who was tormented for eternity by fruit just beyond his reach.) Well, as extreme as this sounds, that's exactly what can happen if our values are out of line.

As an achievement-oriented person, tangible goals gave me a sense of direction, purpose, meaning, and validation. All throughout my life, I've tailored my activities to reach certain goals. That has always been how I located my place in the world. If I achieved my goal, I earned validation and a greater sense of worth. When I was a swimmer, a tennis player, a field hockey player and a golfer, I could tell I was on the right path when I was rushing toward a particular outcome—the championship race, the match, the tournament, or the lowest score in a round of 18 holes. When I played piano, my goal was getting ready for the annual recital and memorizing the piece I would play for my audience of parents and peers. In my academic career, it was the final exam and the final grade that validated my efforts (or sent me off in a downward spiral of self-criticism, if it didn't go so well).

Tangible goals were easy to follow because they did the work of guiding me. They were like a road map. By referring to them, I always knew where I was going and when I had either arrived or become lost along the way. I knew how to feel about this kind of map I thought I could trust. They brought validation and purpose and direction.

No matter how hard I pushed, at times I couldn't shake that feeling of something being out of line. It would just linger around everything in my life like a smoke. Many of my clients, too, report that they have this kind of experience. Despite the success, there is a pervasive feeling of being off or out of step or out of alignment or frustrated or disappointed or just kind of blah. It's as bewildering to them as it was to me. All outward signs in their lives point to happiness and success. And yet those feelings don't occur as expected. It's taken me years to figure out where that sense of disappointment or 'off-ness' came from, and now, after experiencing it again and again, I know what it is and how to prevent it.

To understand why this happens and how we can prevent it in the future, we have to look at what are called Core Values. Our Core Values are those things in life that are most important to us. They are manifestations of our innermost compass that helps to keep us centered in our identity and focused on being our best selves. When any of our core values are not being honored, we feel like we've veered off course. Or we feel just plain frustration. Sometimes the feeling may be slight and other times we feel deep disappointment and irritation even while achieving great things. Either way, when that dissatisfied feeling is there, it's *there...* And no matter how much you achieve or distract yourself by pressing forward to your goal, it won't leave you.

That feeling deep in your gut is immeasurably important because it tells you that something vital in life is missing. No matter how great the success, if it comes at the cost of a Core Value or it is just simply out of line with a Core Value, then the success will not be all that satisfying. When your Core Values are being honored— when you are letting them guide your course—you will notice the difference in your experiences of success. You will be living the life that is most important to *you* not a life that just pleases others or seems to be fulfilling on paper. When we have this feeling of disappointment or just being 'off,' it often stems from what is important to us being in conflict with what is happening around us in the moment. I know this because it happened to me.

Let me explain.

Years ago, I was traveling extensively for my Global Sales Leader job. I loved the adventure and freedom associated with traveling, but what I was missing was my connection to the people I loved. Yes, I was connected to my team in different parts of the world, but as a single mom, I was missing out on quite a bit of the time I could have been spending with my son. At first, I loved the job and the people, but then as the trips continued and I missed more days and nights with my son, I realized something was "off." I began to project that feeling of discomfort outward toward everything around me in the company.

Eventually, I grew to resent the company for not having a local office. I resented the manufacturing plant for missing shipments and for having quality-control problems, which obligated me to organize yet another flight and a customer visit. I was getting frustrated with the airlines for having delayed flights. I was frustrated with the bad weather. I found myself frustrated in almost every situation, resentful about the demands of my job, and blaming everyone and everything for my feelings of frustration, feelings of 'off-ness', and my lack of fulfillment. It was terrible for me, and I imagine it was not easy for those around me.

My life felt unfamiliar, like I was trapped in some other body. I just wanted to get back to feeling "normal." The job itself had not changed since I'd started it. It was the same, as were all other noticeable components of my life. What changed were my thoughts about how my life "should" be. My mindset was stuck in those thoughts of what "should" be rather than assessing what *was* and choosing actions that would bring my life back into alignment with my values. I was succeeding within my company. I was achieving greatly as a businesswoman. I was making all the money I wanted! I had met all my tangible goals, but inside of me—at my core—something felt wrong.

My Core Values were not being honored, and I was suffering from it.

Chapter 34

Core Values Explained

I learned about Core Values when I was still in my corporate role as a Global Sales Leader. I was being certified as a professional coach, and I did a Core Values exercise that allowed me to discover which values are most important to me based on where I was in life at the time. I learned that values can change depending on major life circumstances like getting married, becoming a parent, moving into retirement, changing careers, losing a loved one, or committing to a new passion. However, because the exercise really gets to what's most important to you at your heart, your Core Values may not shift much throughout your life. In this way, they are a little like the foundation for a good life. Or, rather, they are like a compass that guides to what is most important to you.

To identify your Core Values, follow the directions below. It is exactly what I use with my clients, and it has the same list of values I refer to in a session.

1. Find a quiet place.
2. Circle 15 words on the list below that mean the most to you in life. Take your time, there's no rush. Just sit with them and circle the most important.
3. Now take those 15 and take away 5 so you are left with the 10 words that mean the most to you. (This is where you may get uncomfortable. It isn't easy to start eliminating items from your list. Remember, there is no right or wrong; the

exercise is for you and based on what is most important to you.)

4. Next, take the 10 words that are left, and take away the 5 that don't mean as much as the others.

5. Congratulations! You are left with your top 5 Core Values!

Values Assessment

Abundance	Decisiveness	Independence	Recognition
Acceptance	Dependability	Individuality	Relaxation
Accomplishment	Determination	Influence	Reliability
Accountability	Discipline	Ingenuity	Reputation
Accuracy	Diversity	Inspiration	Resilience
Achievement	Drive	Integrity	Respect
Adaptability	Education	Intelligence	Responsibility
Advancement	Empathy	Intimacy	Sacrifice
Adventure	Enjoyment	Introspection	Satisfaction
Affection	Environmentalism	Intuitiveness	Security
Affluence	Ethics	Joy	Self-control
Aggressiveness	Excellence	Justice	Self-reliance
Ambition	Fairness	Kindness	Self-respect
Appreciation	Faith	Knowledge	Sensitivity
Assertiveness	Fame	Leadership	Sensuality
Attentiveness	Family	Love	Service
Attractiveness	Fidelity	Loyalty	Simplicity
Balance	Financial	Making a	Sincerity
Beauty	independence	difference	Spirituality
Being the best	Fitness	Meaning	Spontaneity
Belonging	Fortitude	Meekness	Stability
Camaraderie	Freedom	Meticulousness	Status
Candor	Friendliness	Mindfulness	Strength
Capability	Friendship	Modesty	Structure
Charity	Frugality	Motivation	Success
Cheerfulness	Fulfillment	Nature	Support
Commitment	Fun	Open-minded	Sympathy
Community	Generosity	Optimism	Teamwork
Compassion	Grace	Organization	Trustworthy
Competition	Gratitude	Originality	Truth
Confidence	Growth	Partnership	Understanding
Connection	Happiness	Passion	Vision
Consciousness	Harmony	Patience	Warmhearted
Contentment	Health	Peace	Wealth
Control	Helpfulness	Perseverance	Worthiness
Cooperation	Honesty	Popularity	Other_____
Courage	Honor	Power	Other_____
Courtesy	Hopefulness	Privacy	
Creativity	Humility	Professionalism	
Credibility	Humor	Prosperity	

1

Note: To print out the list, you can find it at my website: www.sherrywelsh.com

After I completed this exercise and I realized two of my Core Values, Connection and Integrity, were not being honored by me and others around me within the company, I knew it was time to make a change. I believed I was alone as I traveled the world, missing my son and others I enjoyed spending time with, surrounded by strangers in hotels and airports. At the time, I did not have a coach, nor the understandings about how to question my thoughts around being all alone. So I just let my frustration build and made the decision to leave the company.

Whenever a Core Value is being threatened or not honored in some way, a sense of frustration or helplessness will result. Once you are clear on your Core Values, it becomes really easy to identify what the source of frustration is. It also becomes really easy to take ownership and communicate to others the reason why something is important for you. When you slow down and recognize which value is not being honored by the choices you are making throughout the day, you can course correct to get more aligned with your Core Values and life will flow with more ease.

Chapter 35

Missing Pieces

Sarah came into our session together near her boiling-over point. She, an upper-level management leader for a global sales department, is a mother of two children she absolutely lives for. A ten-year old and little five-year-old, Bobby. In addition to devoting herself to her sons, Sarah had also worked very hard to get to where she was in her company. She had studied hard in college, gone to graduate school, and was blazing her own trail in the corporate world. She loved the work she did, and the team she was a part of. She was fully behind her boss and the strategy he'd laid out for the upcoming year.

In spite of all this success, something felt "off" for her, so we decided to take a closer look at what was going on in her life with the hope of tracking down where this struggle was coming from. I started by investigating what seemed most present for her.

"What's not working right now? What's the trouble?"

"Well, I feel like there's too much to do and not enough time to do it all."

"Tell me more about what 'all' means. What activities make up the 'all'?" This word alone—"all"—demonstrates the stress she was feeling. The pressure to perform well in all areas of her life, and the heaps and heaps of tasks and expectations she felt piling up on her. There is no way to do it "all" (as in everything needing her attention) but in her sped-up, fast-paced thinking, this is how it felt to her. It looked to her like she truly had to be everything to everyone all the time. Her language reflected her mentality, so we dove into that first.

"I love my job and the people I work with, but my boss keeps heaping on work that I can't say no to. Because of that, I don't get out of the office until well past 5 p.m. And by then, I'm tired, and cranky, and I miss giving my kids their bath. I just don't have time to do all that I want to do in a day." Her usually soft voice was now characterized by a sharpness that was clearly a result of the enormous stress and defeat she felt.

"I see. That's a lot of activities to pack into a day." I said, expressing my sympathy. "I can see how there would be some stress building up. Many of the actions we take in a day help us to fulfill something important to us. And when certain actions consume our time and bleed into our personal time, we can deprive ourselves of what's important for us in our private lives." I paused watching for that flash of recognition. "Does this make sense?"

"Yes. It does."

"OK, let's look at your Core Values and see which of these values might not be getting enough time and attention in your life."

"OK, how do we do that?"

I walked her through the exercise I have added in this book, and we discovered her Core Values.

"So what are your Core Values?" I asked.

"Achievement, Family, Financial Independence, Love, Respect," she said with a big smile, like she had found something that was missing.

"Great! Which Core Value is not being honored when you choose to stay in the office well-past five?"

"Family."

"So when a Core Value is not being honored, or when it is threatened in some way, you drop into your fight-or-flight mode, you're in catabolic energy. And if you actually look more closely at the situation, you'll see that you are choosing to be in the office. You are making the choice to favor achievement and financial independence rather than family." I wanted to cut right to the heart of it, so she could see what was happening.

"But I can't say no to my boss!" She said with a little indignation in her voice.

"How true is that, really? Are you an indentured servant? Is he holding a gun?"

"No, but I don't want to make him upset, or lose my job, or lose face, or lose credibility. I am a great employee, and I have to live up to that."

"So what is the worst that would happen, if you did say no to the extra work? What would happen if you chose to also favor your *family* Core Value?"

She paused and thought. Then broke the silence with a slight sigh. "I guess he might be a little frustrated at the prospect that certain tasks wouldn't get done. But if I delegated those, then he'd really have nothing to be upset about." She paused again.

"Whom will you delegate it to?"

"I can give it to Tom. I know he'll be able to handle it."

"Great. So when are you going to test that out? How soon can you create time for your family?"

"Probably tomorrow."

"Probably?" I retorted.

"Okay, Sher. Tomorrow!"

Sarah was able to shift out of her frustration and victim story. She identified what was missing, and took action to make the desired adjustment. What a simple and powerful solution to that feeling of being off. Outwardly she is a huge success, and yet she was neglecting an essential element of her life—her family. And she was doing so because of a false belief. Walking through this Core Values exercise and slowing down to dismantle her limiting beliefs, she was able to course correct, and spend much wanted time with her kids. Needless to say, she's not feeling off about this anymore.

Chapter 36

Loving What You Do

The grass isn't greener on the other side. The grass is
greener where you water it.[*]

I was meeting with my client, Lindsay, the head of
marketing in an automotive company. She was getting a
bit disenchanted with the amount of reporting and
number crunching that goes along with that particular
function in that particular company. She was falling into
the pattern of frustration that comes with having to just
show up and get your work done. She felt disconnected
and out of touch with the company, her role, and her
mission there. She was tired of it all. And this attitude
showed up all day long.

For her to be happier, I wanted to tune back into her
passion for the work she was doing and turn up the
flame within her! Otherwise, she would continually feel
lackluster and listless.

"What's the mission of your company," I started.

"To be the best supplier of seat belts in the
industry," she said.

I yawned in an exaggerated way, making it clear that
this response would bore anyone, especially her. "Who
benefits from the products you make in your company?"
I said, with a bit more vigor in my voice.

---

[*] My colleague and master coach, Lori Richards, captured this
saying she found on a sign in an antique store.

"The drivers and passengers of vehicles."

"Okay. How do they benefit?"

"The seat belts protect them from injury or dying in a crash."

"Now we are getting somewhere," I said. "Great! So basically you help to save lives! What a great thing to be a part of in this world, given the number of accidents happening every day."

She started to open up and become more animated. "Yes!" she said. "I'm proud to be part of what this company does. We really help people."

I asked her to recall her Core Values, the qualities she honors most in this world. "Which Core Values are supported by your company's mission?" I asked her.

"Family, Security, and Peace," she replied easily. "I can imagine my family being safer with our seat belts, and I have peace of mind knowing that they work, that they are of high quality."

"Great! I love it. And seeing that, how does your specific role support the overall mission of the company?"

She paused and reflected on this, while cocking her head to one side. We sat in a short silence together that she broke by telling me about the amount of data that is analyzed and synthesized into meaningful reports for upper management to use.

"How does upper management use the information your team generates?" I asked, getting her to slow down and really observe what she was saying.

"Easy. To make decisions."

"What kind of decisions?"

"I'm not sure," she said a little hesitantly.

"OK... that's good. Let's take a minute to imagine what kind of decisions your data can be used for." We were really slowing down to observe the situation and gain insights.

She thought a minute and then responded. "Well, I believe they use it to decide whether we will produce a particular product based on consumer trends and demand."

"Great! What else?"

"Well, based on the data, they use that information to decide whether we continue producing what we already do... if it's not as high in demand as it used to be, they produce less. Or, if our forecast shows that demand is increasing they decide to make more."

"Awesome. Who is affected by the decisions that get made by upper management based on the data they receive from you and your team?" I asked.

"The manufacturing plants."

"And how does this data influence the manufacturing plants?"

"Well, they may have to lay people off or close a plant down if the data shows the product is not in demand," she said frankly.

"Yes... And what happens to those people?"

"They lose their jobs and may not be able to provide for their families." She was starting to really see where I was going and her compassion and caring continued to rise in our conversation.

"So how important is it for you to be fully focused, engaged, enthusiastic, creative and inspired to show up each day and give it your best to produce quality reports for upper management?"

As she thought about this, I could see her passion growing stronger. "What I do really does make an impact on the world. I help save lives and keep people employed!"

I nodded in agreement! What Lindsay had discovered through this process of Role Clarity was to understand how her current role in the company was not "just a job." It impacts lives. It matters.

Once we had that fire built and stoked, the final step of the exercise was to throw some more fuel on the flames. I had her do some homework. She was to write out three things that she could do to increase her value contribution in her current role. By doing this, she would be able to identify areas where she still had room to grow, rather than seeing the current role as a dead end. She could continue to take steps forward, actions that would remain aligned with her core values. We wanted her to take steps that would energize her with a sense of growth and true contribution.

She came up with some ideas: learning a foreign language that is common in the company, or taking a course at night, or practicing healthy habits, or exercising and walking midday to recharge. Rather than rushing from meeting to meeting, she could work on slowing down, and honoring herself and her time.

.At any point in our career, we can pause, reflect, and consider who is impacted by the work we do. We can take ownership and move toward mastery in whatever phase of life we are in. No matter how long we've been in one company, we can reinvent our relationship with that firm in any given moment. Life is a journey, not a destination! So make the journey an adventure!

Be willing to water the grass where you are. Rather than wanting out, wanting to go to greener pastures, make your current place the greenest pasture. Fully water it. Tend to it. See its value. And then, if after all that, you still know that there is a different place for you to be, get clear on what will take you there. Slow down and tap into your creativity. Then take the first step toward your even better present moment.

Chapter 37

Knowing Your Soul's Journey - or Not

Over the years, I have had many clients tell me, "I just don't know what I'm supposed to be doing with my life." I often hear a familiar desperation in this phrase. The comment comes from a place of longing and frustration that I had throughout some of my career in the corporate world. It caused me pain, this idea that I was severed from my path.

There are some simple solutions to this concern. When someone is hung up on knowing their soul's journey, I will often ask, "When have you been most satisfied in your career? What specifically were you doing? Who were you surrounded by?" I ask these questions so we can attempt to recreate a similar experience and find more joy in the present.

Sometimes, I'll ask my client to tell me about an experience in which time stood still. "What were you doing in those moments?" I'll ask. Usually we can find something worth repeating this way. We can find their state of flow.

Another approach to this 'dilemma' is to look at volunteer opportunities that are attractive to the client or examine the person's Core Values to make sure they are all being met.

All of these can help. All are useful and worth trying.

But more often than not, , people carry with them a belief that they "should" be doing something else, something more important, something massive. And this belief is how desperation seeps in.

What if it is not necessary to "know" your soul's journey? What if that concept is just an overly romantic idea that we use to cause strife and longing in the present moment? What if it's an idea that has us hiding from reality in the safe but distant comfort of fantasy or daydreaming? What if life is much more interesting and wild than that? What if life—rather than having one single, hidden purpose laid out for us—is about discovering many things we love?

What if it's all about experimenting, taking risks, committing to something to see if you like it? What if it's okay to not know what you're "supposed" to be doing with your life? What if what you're currently doing is exactly what you're supposed to be doing? What if you were not meant to be anywhere else besides where you are right now in this moment? You could still change your course at any time, but wouldn't that take the pressure off?

This book has been about slowing down to allow clarity, creativity and your inner-knowing to surface. There is nothing to figure out. Many times we get so hung up on goals, targets, plans, figuring it out, that we miss the true purpose of what we're here to experience. We're here to slow dance with the universe. That's it. When we slow down, let go of controlling the world, take ownership of our current experiences, take ownership of our choices throughout the day, moment by moment, we can enjoy the dance.

That's why this book has the word "ways" in its subtitle. There is no one single path. No one size fits all approach. Take from it what you can learn and apply it. Then carry on.

Chapter 38

Higher Performer: Know Your Limitations

Rebecca called me one day in total exasperation. She had been at her new job for about two months and thought she should have it all figured out by now. Life was spiraling out of control as she strung together 16-hour day after 16-hour day. Desperate, and ready to quit, she was at the end of her rope. Here's how our coaching session went.

"This isn't the right place for me," she blurted out, only a second after I said hello. "I worked 16 hours on Friday and have another 16 hours of work to do this weekend."

Her mind was moving a million miles a second. Her speech was quick and pressured.

"Let's slow it down for a minute…" I suggested. I wanted to get down to what had caused this situation, to guide her attention to the root of the trouble, rather than the surface issues. "Over the last week, what has changed in the scope of your job that's taken you from 9- or 10-hour days to 16-hour days?"

"That's just the way it is around here," she said with the same strain in her voice as before. "My learning curve is taking longer than I thought it would. My boss is trying to take on some of the workload for me, but his boss is not happy that I am not up to speed and able to do the work by myself."

"OK…" I said, taking an audible breath. "Help me understand this… what are the expectations you are trying to meet?"

"I am expected to work these long hours to get the job done. They tell me that's what the people who had this job before me did for their first year in this position. I can't do this for a full year. It's crazy!"

"I agree. It's not sustainable. It's not healthy. People aren't designed to work like that," I responded, taking a short pause before asking, "What were the agreements you made when you interviewed and accepted this job?"

"Well, we talked about what is needed when deadlines loom, and I agreed I would do whatever it took to be a team player and meet the deadlines."

Like many of my clients, she cared. She wanted to succeed and do well by her boss and her company. She wanted to be seen as the leader she could be. In her current state of thinking, though, she wasn't going to make progress.

"OK… what clarity did you get from your boss during the interview as to how often it happens that deadlines are tight and late nights become an everyday occurrence?"

"He made it seem like these stretches were not a regular occurrence, but that I could expect them every so often." Her words shot through with indignation. "But after I got the job, he said that late nights *are* commonplace, that these tight deadlines *are* the norm. He couldn't say that in the interview or no one would want the job!"

"Wow… that sounds a bit out of integrity. No wonder you're both frustrated and exhausted. It makes sense that you feel this way, given the fact that the team leaders are all living in crisis mode, and you're not seeing an end in sight."

"Exactly! I think I should just quit. I can't take this anymore," she said, exhaling.

"Well, that's one option," I said, not wanting her to lose the momentum to make a change. "There are other options, too. If you're willing to explore them, let's take a look."

"OK. I'm not seeing them now, but I'll play along."

"Great! We've identified your Core Values through the Values Assessment you did. Tell me again what they are." (Core Values are the values you hold most important for living a full life.)

"Balance, Growth, Love, Connection, Fun."

"Fantastic! So based on the Core Values you just mentioned, can you see how most, if not all of them, are *not* being honored in your current situation at work?"

"Yes! And I don't see it changing anytime soon." Her cadence had begun to slow down to her regular pace, but I still sensed tiredness and frustration coming through in her language.

"Yes, that would make sense. When that many of your core values are threatened, it's normal to feel helpless and to want to pull back. To retreat. It's a fight or flight response, and you've readied yourself to flee to a place of safety! With 16-hour work days, your balance is way off. Life is not very fun. You have no time to see friends and nurture connection with them, and you're too tired to grow! It certainly won't feel like love when you feel like escape is necessary!"

I paused for a second, as she uttered out a short agreement. I could picture her nodding with the phone to her ear. "It seems like all five of your core values are under attack."

"Oh... I get that. It's true." A slight warmth started coming through the receiver. She was softening, as she began to understand the situation more.

"Given that the current situation is not conducive to honoring any of your Core Values, let's revisit what made you decide to take this job in the first place. Let's relate them to your core values."

"Well, I wanted to be part of a team that was hard-working and smart, which provides *connection*. I also *loved* and believed in the brand I'd be representing. I enjoy the product personally, and thought it would be *fun* to be a part of the company that makes it. I wanted to have an experience I never had and taste the culture, which is a form of *growth*. I also thought I could utilize my skills in project management to launch new products here. That last thing helps me feel *growth and balance*." The excitement she once had for the job was clear, even if it was clouded slightly by the situation.

"I love it! It makes sense why you accepted the job offer and were excited to be a part of this large, complex, multi-cultural, global business!" She was coming with me out of injury and into possibility. Moving from a catabolic state to an anabolic one.

"Yes, and I still see the great possibilities here... maybe just not in this group that I'm a part of now." There was some resignation in her tone, but calmness and understanding replaced the jagged edges of stress that had colored her speech before.

"That could be. Since you've only been there a short time, it's possible that you haven't experienced the ebbs and flows most businesses have. How open are you to sharing your Core Values with your boss? You could help him see what a conflict it is for you to continue with the current schedule. You could give a conversation with him a chance, and use this as an opportunity to connect with your boss and strengthen your relationship."

"I can do that. I *want* to do that for my own well-being and for the company. I will speak with him first thing Monday morning!"

Chapter 39

The Super Employee

What Rebecca and I hadn't covered in that phone call is worth mentioning now. She was placing expectations on herself that helped to create this whole situation. She had saddled herself with the belief that she had to be a perfect employee, one who is able to handle any and every task thrown on her desk, no matter the demands on her time and energy. This caused her to agree to take on an unreasonable amount of work. She wanted to be a great employee, so she kept saying yes to any project her boss put in front of her.

Obviously, this approach doesn't work! The stressed out, burnt out woman on the phone was not functioning at her best. Trying to meet these impossible expectations caused her performance to suffer. The projects entrusted to her, then, were subpar when done. Her overachieving attitude backfired.

The key to maintaining the high performance state is to not overload yourself. Create empowering agreements instead. That is almost always the lesson when dealing with overwhelming obstacles. When you are clear on what is possible for you to deliver with high quality and integrity, within a given work day, your value to the organization and your performance increase accordingly. Co-creating agreements with your boss and co-workers will help maintain a manageable workload for any given time frame. Of course, there are times when extra effort and hours may be required, but it should be the exception, not the norm!

To actually be a high performer—a super employee—doesn't mean to be superhuman. Know your limitations. Know what you can and can't do while producing good work. Integrity comes from win-win agreements, and if you suffer too much, so does all your work. And so does the company and the company's customers. To be a super employee, just be a human who co-creates agreements!

Chapter 40

Money Does Grow on Trees

My mother used to say, "Money doesn't grow on trees." As well intentioned as she was in saying this, she was inadvertently teaching me to have a scarcity mindset. She was teaching me that money is hard to come by. And though our family was well off, she truly lived this belief. To this day, I remember her carefully rinsing and then laying out used paper towels on a drying rack so we could use them again.

Though her efforts may seem like progressive "green" thinking, she wasn't attempting to save the planet. She was simply trying to protect our savings and our family income. To protect her family from the financial scarcity she feared. An idea that was handed down to her from her parents, who lived through the Great Depression years of the 1930s.

My father, too, had these beliefs in his own ways. Yet, somehow, despite what they were teaching me, I was able to get a great education, play sports, take piano lessons, take vacations with my family every year, and so on. We weren't broke. We were just fine. Better than fine. It seemed money somehow always appeared, even if we were taught that it was not easy to come by.

These scarcity beliefs that I adopted were not created by my parents singlehandedly. Their parents, too, taught them how to regard money. Rare. Precious. Fleeting. And just like me, they carried their parents' beliefs, adopted them as their own, and harbored them. Then lived according to their constraints.

That said, these beliefs were not actually representative of reality, however real they felt. As a child, of course, this was difficult, because children internalize their parents' teachings undigested, unconsciously or without processing them. But as an adult, I came to understand that, whenever I wanted, I could adopt beliefs that were different from my parents' beliefs.

Once I started to really live in accordance with the belief that money is actually abundant, I saw evidence of that everywhere.

Chapter 41

My Abundant Life

When I went to college, I got my first credit card. I ran up a few hundred dollars on it with a sneaky trip to Colorado to visit friends. I was afraid to tell my parents about this debt and to ask for their help. Letting them know I had incurred money troubles only seemed like it would make things worse!

Besides, I figured that if I paid the minimum $10 payment each month, the problem would go away. Of course, paying the minimum amount due didn't help at all. After several months, I hadn't paid the debt off! No one explained to me that the $10 minimum barely paid for the interest gained on the original balance. The base just continued to grow each month as it gained more interest. I had no idea that would happen. Eventually, my back was against a wall, and I had to find work to dig myself out of this hole.

I mustered up the courage and got a job washing hair in a beauty salon during my senior year of college in Easton, Pennsylvania. The job was humbling. Terrible, actually. But it taught me that I could find ways to pay the bills even if I didn't like the job. I also learned that I wanted to make a lot more money so I could pay my own bills and *not* have to wash strangers' hair! Even at that point, despite how I felt about my debts, I began to see abundance in my life. I *could* indeed pay my bills. I did have a greater earning capacity than my paycheck indicated. There it was, the thread of abundance weaving through my life.

Higher pay didn't happen for some time, however. I graduated college with a degree in engineering without any internship experience. Worse, I graduated into a national recession, so the job market was tight. No matter how hard I searched, I could not find anything in my field for someone without any internship experience. I had been a lifeguard and a waitress in the summers between my years in college, so I felt like I was left high and dry. Like I had no valuable experience to offer. I was frustrated with myself for not having chosen to do an internship while in college, and the fear of not having money filled me again.

What I didn't appreciate at the time was that the skills I learned while working those summer jobs equipped me for life! Certain skills I learned then provided me with deep abundance years later!

While waitressing at a 5-Star Dude Ranch in Colorado, I learned the art of excellent customer service, which requires great attention to detail. By learning to be very attentive to the needs of the guests I served, I learned to anticipate customers' requests. Moreover, I learned that the size of my tip and my pay ultimately came down to one thing—how deeply I connected with and served my customers. What a strong lesson. This concept is actually at the heart of prosperity, I know that now. When we offer supreme service, we get abundance back.

I learned to support my customers, listen to them, and ensure that their every request was heard and addressed appropriately.

Years later, my customer service skills became the backbone of my success in sales when I was in the automotive industry. I could help my team and customers by anticipating their needs with care and attention, while making sure every detail of a program or negotiation was appropriately addressed. These skills still apply to my career today! As a coach, my ability to connect with my clients and anticipate their needs is vital. It's the foundation for my success. And theirs.

Everything I learned about helping people came down to one powerful insight about abundance. When I was working at my best—operating at my highest level—money wasn't the object of my work. In fact, my job was simple: bring as much value as possible to the lives of others. And in doing so, money naturally followed.

Wealth, it turns out, is a byproduct of deep and valuable service. This means that the secret to making money is not like stumbling upon a goldmine and then hoarding what comes out. Money actually is very easy to come by when what you are putting out into the world is of great value to others. Money is energy. It's flowing always. It's a choice where people spend it. It just takes adding deep, meaningful value to the world and developing systems that reward this value.

When I think back to my mother's comments about money, I have empathy for her and where her concern was coming from. I know she was teaching me what she thought would be best, even though it was a disempowering belief. And when I think about it now, I actually get a kick out of it, at how wrong she was. Money does actually grow on trees —it's made out of paper, which comes from trees! Or, can you picture this? A forest of trees all dangling twenties? Millions of dollar bills in different colors littering the ground as fall arrives? Then there is the species of tree that issues torrents of hundreds from its low-hanging branches! It sounds like fantasy, but the truth is we all live here, in this forest of abundance.

If only my mother took a minute to slow down her automatic beliefs, question them, and look around, maybe she'd be seeing all the green that grows around us!

What I love working on with clients today is asking the questions; "Given the belief you created from your parents' views on money, how true is that belief for you today? How well is that belief working for you? What belief would you like to create instead?" Though it seems too easy to be true, these few questions really can make a massive difference in your life, as long as you follow them up with immediate action. In other words: What is the first step you need to take in order to strengthen your new, chosen belief?

Now, take that step!

Chapter 42

A Foundation for Self-Coaching

Albert Einstein once said, "Energy cannot be created or destroyed, it can only be changed from one form to another." How true this is for each of us in regards to emotional energy. Emotional energy cannot be created or destroyed. We carry it with us all day, and it has the ability to move us between varying states of confidence and productivity or self-doubt and conflict, just to name a few. All day, we shift between various states along a spectrum of emotional energy.

On the one side of this spectrum is the catabolic energy, which is toxic, draining, exhausting. The other pole is constituted by anabolic energy, which is freeing, uplifting, inspiring, creative. Along this spectrum, between the two poles, there are actually seven distinct states, or seven levels of energy, each with its own characteristics. While coaching, I often refer to these seven levels to help my clients identify their energy levels so that they can take ownership of their lives in the moment. Having knowledge of the seven levels of energy is in itself very freeing for my clients. It demonstrates that an emotional state, no matter how painful or frustrating or deeply rooted, is actually temporary and influenced by thought. Moreover, when we slow down to identify these states as they come up, we can swing between them easily by making certain decisions in the moment. And therein lies the power. We can become owners of our lives in an instant, going from feeling stuck to feeling free as quickly as an electric charge can pass through our neurons.

In the book *Energy Leadership* by Bruce D. Schneider, the founder of iPEC Coaching and the creator of the Core Energy Coaching process, the author explains that on the one side of this spectrum is catabolic energy, which is toxic, draining, and exhausting. The other pole is made of anabolic energy, which is freeing, uplifting, inspiring, creative.

A succinct way to characterize Schneider's 7 Levels of energy is below, starting from most catabolic and ending with most anabolic:

- Level 1: Victim (Poor Me / Retreat = Flight)
- Level 2: Fighter (I'm Right, You're Wrong = Fight)
- Level 3: Rationalizer (Let's Move Forward = Cooperate)
- Level 4: Care Giver (Make Easy for Others)
- Level 5: Partner (True Win-Win)
- Level 6: Visionary (Being in Flow)
- Level 7: Creator (Pure Creation)

My clients use the following chart as a reminder to see how our options become limited and our energy levels drop when in the lower states. And vice-versa: how options become plentiful and energy remains high when in the higher states.

The 7 Levels of Energy Leadership

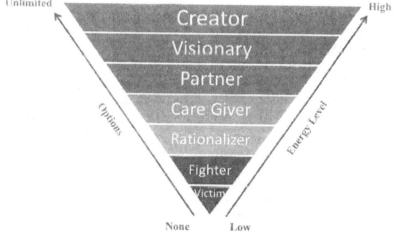

Here's an example of the way these levels of thinking show up in real life. Let's say you're a salesperson in a large company. And your customer calls on Saturday morning telling you the plant did not ship the parts it promised. Your customer is infuriated, and starts to tell you that they may have to shut down their production line, because these parts aren't there yet. The customer says your company will probably be liable for the lost profits.

So, what do you think about this situation? It depends.

The Level 1 in you might sound like this: *Oh, man. Not again. That plant never ships on time.*

The Level 2 in you might sound like this: *Are you kidding me? Again? The plant manager should be fired!*

Level 3: *Well... the plant must have a reason. I will get them on the phone and come up with a plan to fix this immediately.*

Level 4: *They must be overwhelmed there... I wonder how I can help them. I will pull together a conference call and ask them what we can do to help them get it turned around.*

Level 5: *This is a great opportunity to have all the key players come together and create agreements on how to resolve this quickly and determine what obstacles we can jointly remove to ensure this same issue doesn't happen again.*

Level 6: *I'm going to stay in the moment and allow my intuition to guide and be creative for a quick and effective idea. I know we will all learn something valuable from this experience. How can I continue to slow down to find the right answers to address this* situation? How can we generate an ideal set of agreements going forward?

Level 7: *Life is good... And life is exactly as it's meant to be. I can create the experience I choose from this.*

You can apply these 7 Levels to just about any situation, and you may respond to a similar situation in completely different ways, depending on what state you are in and what choices you're making in your life in that specific moment. The higher levels of energy are pretty rewarding and generative, so let's look at the ways we land in lower energy states. That way you can start to make progress by noticing when you get in these states, minimizing the amount of time you stay in them and shifting out of them more quickly.

Chapter 43

How We Land in Victimhood

All of us wander back and forth between these levels. Some of us are more unconscious of the factors that influence our shifts between energetic states. We remain unaware of the fact that we have the power to choose what state we want to occupy even if we are exposed to a certain external trigger. Instead of actively choosing what state we want to be in, we often continue to react to what we believe life throws at us. However, we do have the power to choose which Energy Level we operate from. We can open up to the benefits of each of these states and make choices about how we respond to any given situation we find ourselves in throughout the day. We can move from perceiving ourselves as victims of life's circumstances to defining ourselves as leaders. In order to understand how, we'll first need to take a look at some of the primary culprits that compel us into a catabolic state.

All of our emotional states come directly from what thoughts and beliefs we hold, whether negative or positive. There are some external triggers that can lead us to disempowered states as well, such as an intensely threatening situation or trauma, the amount of exercise we do, how much sleep we get, the emotional state of those we spend time with, what types of foods we put into our bodies, how well we attend to our spiritual beliefs. All these factors can influence our energy levels. For instance, if we are spending time with negative people, eating poorly, and never exercising, our energy levels are most likely lodged in a catabolic state. The opposite might be true if we are taking care of ourselves, laughing with others, and attending to our physical well being. There are many, many books about diet and sleep and exercise and spiritual practices and the impact of those around us, so do check some out.

This book, however, focuses on addressing the internal elements, the beliefs and thoughts that we have and how these lead to directly to our emotional states. Throughout this book you find many beliefs and attitudes and thoughts that lead people to Victim Energy, and you are seeing how the shifts in their thinking helped them come out of this. To warm you up to these concepts, here are some of the thoughts and beliefs that lead one into this disempowering territory. Our thoughts, after all, shape so much of our world.

~ Dwelling on past failures is an easy route to victimhood. When we continually recall the feeling of shame that resulted from missing a deadline, for instance, or when we mentally rehearse a shoddy sales conversation, we stay stuck in a catabolic state. How easy it is to fall into a depressive mood or a self-critical mode when we focus on "how bad" we have done before. And the more focus and attention we give this past experience, the more helpless we feel and the more deeply we root ourselves in Victim Land.

~ Certain beliefs we are taught from our parents, teachers, and other experts can become internalized and foundational in the way we see the world and what's possible, or not possible. You see in this book, how I explain certain limiting beliefs I adopted from my parents about money and my dream job of teaching. Because I looked up to my parents as the authority and experts, and because I didn't know another worldview as a child, it was very easy for me to adopt their beliefs.

Certain attitudes I learned from them held me back from pursuing my passion to teach, and the more I repeated again and again the belief that money is scarce, the more strongly this idea took hold of me. They thought they were helping me by passing these ideas down to me, and my unconscious acceptance of these beliefs had me hold back and stay in Victim Land longer than I would have liked.

~ Another way into the catabolic energy of victimhood is assuming that past experiences dictate future or present moments. That is, we can spend time in our minds predicting what terrible thing could happen again, even though the current situation is completely unique. I had once given a suboptimal presentation years ago, while at Bosch, and for months afterward, before each next presentation I kept thinking about this past experience and imagining how humiliating it was going to be to fail again. This kind of false predictive power only led me to greater anxiety and struggle.

~ We can find a quick route to Victim Land when we have a belief or story that someone doesn't like us, or someone doesn't listen to us, or someone doesn't trust us. When we spend time trying to read someone else's mind, often we don't come up with the most empowering or constructive stories. With the perspective that someone doesn't like us, we can easily descend into a low state, we can start to people please, grasp for approval, or just clam up and withdraw. In this state, we are often crippled and knotted up, leaving little freedom to take constructive action.

~ The most powerful internal force driving people to feeling like helpless victims is the sharp barbs of the inner critic, that little gremlin we all have tucked away in our minds. This particular pattern of thought tries to keep us safe, but often it completely undercuts or distorts our true capabilities. I have seen many brilliant people burn themselves out and live way below their capacity when they listen to the damaging influence of this voice.

~ This "protective" gremlin shows up in phrases like, "I could never do that." Or, "I am not experienced enough and I don't know enough." Or, "No one ever listens to me." Or, "I always end up making a massive mistake." Pay particular attention to the words "never" and "always," because these are utter distortions. How can someone know if they can never do something? Is it actually always true that people never listen to you? These distortions lead to very painful living.

~ When our Core Values are threatened, we can get caught up in Level 1 (Victim) or Level 2 (Fighter) states. Our relationships, our sense of meaning in life, and our decisions are all anchored in what we call Core Values. These are things like integrity, family, loyalty, financial independence, connection with others, empathy, and generosity, to name a few. When another person, a situation, or even ourselves is not honoring one of our Core Values, we will either retreat or fight to protect ourselves from harm. Hence, we head straight to Level 1 or Level 2 energy as a result.

Recall the story about the client of mine, Cindy, who was suffering tremendously balancing life and work. Her pain came from the fact that she thought two of her core values—family and career success—were competing for her time and energy. In her mind, she couldn't successfully do both without causing greater burnout! At the end of the day, exhausted, she would leave the job she loved and then overextend herself to please her children, which led to even more stress. This all shifted for her as we brainstormed in the session and developed alternative ideas for her to enjoy time with both her family and her clients.

Chapter 44

Women's Lodgings in Victim Land

As I've seen in my life and the lives of my clients, there are many major factors that cause women to hang out in catabolic energy states for longer than desired. Here is a list that is not comprehensive, but thorough nonetheless.

~ Allowing our natural feminine characteristic of caring and nurturing others to extend too long, without caring for ourselves, can hold us in a catabolic state. As strange as this sounds, depending on how it's done and for how long, taking care of or nurturing others can either hinder you or help you. To not play the role of caretaker can go against the instinct of many of my clients, as many are compassionate and service-oriented. In some of the dialogues in the book, you've seen the ways they can be both nurturing and empowering to themselves and others, when they approach the situation with their Level 5 (Partner) thinking.

~ Women can be socially conditioned to be more reserved and to put others ahead of themselves. Many are not taught or encouraged to ask for what they want. They wait for recognition from others and tend to hang back rather than propelling themselves forward. These habits can lead to resentment and frustration that result in Level 2 (Fighter) energy. Worse, these socially conditioned habits can lead to deep and lasting frustration and marginal personal and career success. Putting one's own wants and ambitions last can be frustrating and depressing, leaving one far from thriving!

~ Some women accept being passed over for promotions or other opportunities for success because they are told that they're "needed" where they are. It feels good to be needed. Out of a sense of duty, they continue to wait their turn, and as a result they feel helpless (Level 1/Victim) and can shift into feeling resentment over time (Level 2/Fighter).

~ When women compare themselves to others or to some artificial and extreme standard, they begin to seek a false and unattainable idea of perfection. Because these standards are an illusion—and exist strictly in our own imaginations—they cause many women to experience frustration and disempowerment. Comparison reinforces beliefs and feelings of unworthiness and worthlessness, leaving them feeling not good enough or inadequate in some way. This is where the "Inner-critic" just loves to take hold and wreak greater havoc on one's emotional well-being. Who doesn't know the sting of that inner voice and its barbs even just a little?

~ Many of my clients, like me, have learned to fit into the male culture in their companies, and as a result have lost touch with their feminine qualities. They submerge and repress many of their natural instincts, and so they feel tense, stressed out and overworked. They become too aggressive and feel at odds with themselves. Not balancing masculine and feminine traits in a way that suits the individual can certainly lead someone into a catabolic state.

Do any of these apply to you? Have you ever found yourself being too nurturing? Too self-sacrificing? Or, conversely, have you ever found yourself feeling out of touch with your feminine side? Have you found yourself feeling too aggressive and disconnected from your instincts? Have you ever been stuck in a mode of comparison? Judging yourself or feeling jealous because you don't "measure up" to someone else in your life?

If that is the case for you, I totally get it. I have been there myself many times. And I have spent many hours learning how to leave these habits behind. Once you have a greater understanding of events that trigger stress and land you in catabolic states, you will be able to make choices in your life that lead to ownership. As you slow down and increase your awareness, you will begin to recognize when Level 1 (Victim) and Level 2 (Fighter) can creep in, and you will then be conscious of the choice you have to shift to more productive, creative, and empowering anabolic levels.

From there, great progress can be made. You can step out of victimhood and into ownership just by asking simple questions in the moment.

Ask yourself:

- *Who am I being right now, which Level of Energy am I behaving from?*
- *How can I acknowledge and validate myself to allow understanding to surface?*
- *What is a different perspective I can take regarding this situation?*
- *What is a more empowering belief to have about the circumstances?*
- *What is a more productive way to think about this situation?*
- *I wonder what's going on for them?*

- *How would my Level 5 (Partner) or Level 6 (Visionary) deal with this situation?*
- *How would my Level 7 (Creator) view this situation?*

The answer to these questions may not come immediately, though with practice you will quickly learn how to use this kind of self-coaching. You will see its benefits and just how quickly it can change your experience of any given situation.

When we start to question and replace the negative thoughts that lead to a catabolic state, we find it much easier to shift out of the negative and disempowered or angry state. We can get into constructive action, and that will help us leave the stress behind. We can form and then take clear steps toward better relationships, better work habits, and better self-care. Just slowing down and questioning your thinking, and actively seeking better, more empowering questions, will help move you into higher energy levels. The simple act of not responding immediately to a negative impulse or idea will help you create more ease in your day-to-day living. It will make you a creative owner of each moment!

Chapter 45

Shifting Out of Victim Land

Monica's stress was palpable; it filled the room before she even sat down and said a word.

"I don't know what I'm going to do... My boss asked me to meet with the new VP of Sales and I'm not sure why."

She was merely reacting to the situation presented to her. So she felt stuck, like a bystander in her own life. She was deep in her Level 1 (Victim) energy. I wanted her to see that she had choices in the matter—that she was an active participant in creating her reality.

"Well, how about you ask him what the purpose of the meeting is and how he believes you will benefit by meeting with him," I said, urging her to strive for clarity.

"I did, but he didn't give me anything concrete," she responded desperately.

"I would like you to practice not leaving a conversation with your boss until you are satisfied that the direction he wants you to go is clear," I said, giving her a strategy that would bring her to a more anabolic energy, a place of ownership and co-creation, Level 5 - Partner energy. "When you allow your boss to be evasive and not answer your questions with enough precision, then it is on you to continue to ask for clarity. Otherwise, you'll stay stuck in victimhood and your lower energy levels, which, of course, are not all that productive for you or your team."

"OK, I get that," she said while beginning to slow down her breathing. "But I don't know why I have to go to Chicago to meet the new guy when my boss is the one who will be interacting with him more than I will." She was still responding as if she was powerless.

"That sounds like an assumption you're making," I said, wanting her to see that she was still in Level 1 (Victim) thinking. "Where does that come from?"

"Well, that's how it's always been," she replied. Her body language was still stiff and uncomfortable. "The upper management never interacts with anyone on my level."

"So, given that upper management has not interacted with you much in the past, it makes sense you're frustrated and confused by your boss's request," I responded with an Acknowledge and Validate to shift her a bit into her Level 3 (Rationalizer/Cooperation) energy in order to create some mutual understanding and connection.

"See, you get it now!" she exclaimed as she shifted to meet me at Level 3, which brought her out of Level 1 (Victim) mode, at least temporarily.

"It does make total sense that you feel this way, based on your previous experience. Since it's now a new situation with new people involved, what kind of relationship would you like to create with this new VP that would help you perform even better in your current role?" This question was the crux of her shift to empowerment in this situation.

"Hmmm… that's a good question…" She was relaxing into her chair and moving into a state of ownership, scaling the Levels to a Level 6 (Visionary). Then, from this new place of power, she found her answer. "I would like to see a regular interaction with this new guy that includes my ideas for a global customer strategy and future market penetration for certain products in different parts of the world," she said. "We've been so conservative with our technology introductions over the years. This could be my chance to really make a difference by having a powerful relationship with the top guy!"

Finally Monica was articulating her desires and crafting a plan with confidence. She was moving from a stuck and shutdown state into a state of creative, productive thinking and ideas for action. All she had to do was slow down to see that she was not actually a victim in this situation. She could slow down and see that she is an owner, creative and powerful in each moment.

Certain aspects of human nature, our very biological impulses, it seems, can drag us to disempowered states of mind. The fight or flight response for instance—one of the most basic survival instincts—instantly propels many of us into a catabolic state. Gender does not discriminate in this case. When a threat is perceived, women and men have equal access to this catabolic level, though on an individual level we each respond slightly differently to stress stimuli. I have worked with some clients who experience very little Level 1 (Victim) energy and very high Level 2 (Fighter) energy under stress. I also have clients who experience higher Level 1 energy and lower Level 2 energy under stress. The circumstances that trigger stress for each of us are different, but without fail, stress always leads to catabolic states that drain us.

Think about it... When at work you get that mid-morning call with some urgent-sounding coworker, who can barely take a breath as he explains how the big account in Germany is about to fall through. As the conversation progresses and your imaginations take over, you both start to worry more and more.

One avenue you may take to release the worry is turning to some type of escape: alcohol, food, social media, work, gossip, to name a few. Drinking too much, for instance, to blow off steam, and hanging out with the party animals might feel good temporarily, but it will drain you in the long term. Trust me, I know. I was there. I loved to have 'fun' and enjoy the sweet release of alcohol, yet the troubles that came with it began to be overwhelming. Why? I was not attending to my well being and so I sank into a regular catabolic state, which, of course, led me to want more wine! When we slow down and nurture ourselves—rather than turn to something outside of us to escape the stress and worry—we'll be able to function at an optimal level of energy and not get caught in a depleting cycle of catabolic energy.

Chapter 46

Can This Thinking Really Bring Release?

"Let's go have a drink!"

This was such a common phrase in the corporate world I was a part of, whether uttered to oneself or to a coworker. For many of us, drinking to escape was hardly even regarded as a guilty pleasure, but more like a spoil of war. It was the reward for a hard day's work.

The problem is that drinking in this way reinforces the cycle that some are using the drink to escape from in the first place. At least that was the case for me and for some of my more honest clients.

The activity of drinking to escape comes from victim thinking. This kind of drinking makes the day out to be some kind of battle that one can only retreat or slip away from. Raise the white flag and admit defeat. The act of drinking, which is the act of anesthetizing the mind, only reinforces this mentality, because it keeps you in a continual state of bondage to the feelings that drive you to drink in the first place. Rather than responsibly processing the events of the day or taking ownership of what happened, drinking as an escape, a retreat, becomes a powerful commitment to the idea that life's onslaught is just too overwhelming a foe.

My life, at times, revolved around alcohol. I started drinking regularly in college, like many young people do when first experiencing freedom from home. However, that so-called "social drinking" became a habit that I repeated *every* day for 25 years. The only exception to this daily routine was the short time I was undergoing fertility treatments before we eventually adopted my son. Otherwise, you could find me leaning on this chemical crutch every single day.

Anything that disrupted the pattern alcohol maintained in my life would lead me instantly to irritation and anger. Exercise, healthy eating, getting proper rest, even human connections all took a backseat to my desire for alcohol. At the time, I believed it was the only thing helping me cope with the demands of life. I believed it made me feel better.

My evenings looked like this: I would get home from a long day at work feeling exhausted, park myself on the couch or a chair at the kitchen table, and pour myself a nice glass of red wine. The bitter reward for all I'd been through that day. One glass would easily turn into two, which would turn into three, which would... well, you get the point. Then, in this way, alcohol became the lynchpin to my personal enjoyment of the night. It became the most essential thing I needed to relax and put whatever stress I had experienced behind me for a few hours.

If I needed to attend a party or take my son to football practice or a to a friend's house or go shopping or attend to an errand, the drinking would somehow have to be accounted for in the course of that evening. And, obviously, it's hard to fit in drinking with most of these activities. Inevitably, something would be pushed out of my schedule so that I could drink that night. I had earned that glass of wine, after all.

It hardly needs to be said, but I'll point it out anyway. In this state, I was not connected at all to my environment, the people around me, my responsibilities as a parent and a friend, and the loving connections I truly wanted to nurture. I was self-absorbed and in a state of victimhood, nursing my perceived wounds from the day with however many glasses of wine I felt the injuries merited. I wasn't really even connected to the present moment itself. In fact, the only thing I was connected to was the glass of wine and the *disconnection* it brought me. I would lean forward into the drink that waited for me, my body holding me to the reality of each moment, while my mind wandered to the evening. If I was physically present, all the rest of me was elsewhere.

Being removed from the present moment actually brought even more pain into my life. More of the pain I was trying to escape through drinking. I just didn't know that at the time, because I was numbed to the signs our bodies give us when we are living with awareness. The present is where I make decisions to improve my life, and being severed from that place of existence disables me from wielding the power of choice. The life I really wanted, a life of fulfilling relationships and true happiness, was traded for temporary relief and disconnect.

During the times that I would go out drinking, I had lots of friends. We were all drinking together, and the connection this offered looked good on the surface. Community, clinking glasses, talking about our lives, listening to each other. But in reality, the booze would become a barrier between us. It colored my interactions with everyone I talked to. I had the kind of friends who all drank, and so I embraced the lifestyle that supported that, and part of that lifestyle involved allowing alcohol to think for me. For instance, things happen when you drink large volumes of alcohol, things that wouldn't normally happen. I'd make bad decisions. Cloudy-thinking decisions. I don't need to mention them now, but you can imagine the kind of choices I'm referring to: the kinds that lead to even more trouble.

These bad decisions, of course, led to fallout and the resulting debris of that fallout. Guilt and strained relationships flourish in this environment of self-indulgent behavior. Because we aren't really taking ownership of our choices or our relationships. If I took a look around myself, there was always more to run from, more reasons to escape into that glass. 5 o'clock couldn't come soon enough each day. But for all of the relief 5 o'clock offered, by the next morning, there would probably be another mess to sort through. Which set me right back on the track to ending the day with the reprieve that first drink always gave me.

Even when my friends and I did connect in the chaos, the dialogue wasn't all that constructive or productive or enlightening. It was weighted down with complaints and criticism and indignation and self-pity. We'd listen to each other complain, and the consensus we found would help us build even more stories about how the world had wronged us. The sympathetic person across the table would strengthen the other's sense of injury and anger. No one consciously tried to make the other person upset, but it happened—a lot. These conversations, though, were about wallowing and victimhood. We'd sit together in misery, reinforcing our feelings of defeat and victimization, as our thinking became more and more unclear. (Pull up a chair to my suffering...)

Rather than making empowered decisions to build the lives we really wanted, we'd impair our ability to function optimally. Alcohol alone takes power and clarity from a person, which in and of itself sinks us deeper into the victim state. The conversations were held from one victim to another, and no one had a life raft to offer.

All of these activities, of course, are the opposite of slowing down and connecting with our surroundings. They moved me away from the moment and away from ownership. Mired in self-pity, my friends and I would complain about our circumstances as if there was nothing we could do about them. The only solution seemed to be to have another drink. There is nothing wrong with alcohol. In fact, I still have glass of wine or two with friends or at dinner now and then. But the type of lifestyle I had fallen into when I made heavy drinking my daily ritual was not a recipe for good living, and the alcohol became all tangled up, part and parcel, with the victimhood that brought me so much unnecessary strife.

Chapter 47

Ownership and Alcohol

There was a great *Friends* episode in which Rachel starts smoking cigarettes. She takes up the habit so that she won't be left out of the conversation with her boss and the other woman who was on her team. She doesn't want to miss out when they're out for a smoke break. She doesn't want to be disconnected from either the social interaction or the important discussion they could be having. She wants to be in their social circle, and smoking is the gateway. It's the act that puts them in the same place at the same time, opening an avenue for perceived connection.

Alcohol is often the same thing, right? And it works, at times! As I said, I'm not a reformer, I think alcohol is fine. It is just important to ask some questions about your habits, in order to stay in the ownership state of living.

When you go to a party or happy hour to hang with your friends, family, or coworkers, take a moment to pause. Slow down a minute. Decide what you want to do at this social event, or this party or for this particular evening... Ask, "How do I want to spend this time with these people? What is the outcome I'm hoping for in this particular interaction? Do I want to have a drink or not? If I do, okay, I'm going to have one, because it tastes good with this meal, or I want to celebrate, or I want to be part of the toast, or whatever feels jovial and connected and fun and right in that setting." The idea is to take ownership of the decisions you make throughout the day (and night) rather than being swept up into making decisions that you might not have made had you been clear-headed. Decide what outcome you want *before* you get there. Be intentional.

Make drinking a choice, a ***conscious*** choice each time you decide to imbibe. This is part of the ownership life. Don't just do anything automatically, or because you think you should, drinking included. Be aware of your choices, and be sure that throughout your day, you are dealing with whatever feelings come up, so that the drink, or food, or work, or Facebook, does not need to be a release or a validation for what you've been through that day. It can be just a part of a fun social gathering. Rather than a crutch, it can become a shared experience that doesn't contribute to your life in a negative way

And sometimes, you might happen to have too many drinks, and the next day you'll wake up with those glasses of wine lingering around like the headache or mental fog that's sure to accompany them—just recognize that, too. Don't ignore it because it makes you feel bad, and don't beat yourself up, either. Just notice this decision and its result, and figure out if it serves you and your highest vision. The ownership way of life is all about producing what you most want in the world in the most sustainable ways. It's all about taking control of our choices and enjoying their results, and reflecting on them in ways that are productive and informative.

So let's keep letting go of habits that rob us of our power, shall we? Let's rid the garden of the weeds that are blocking the flowers' growth. Let's focus on feeding and nurturing that flower so that it thrives, rather than inadvertently letting the weeds get all the attention. Let's take ownership.

V.

FULLY FLOURISHING

Chapter 48

Whole-Brain Thinking

When I was an engineer, I was told that I wasn't creative. I understood myself in either/or terms. Either I was a right-brained creative thinker or a left-brained logical thinker. I was told to look at the facts, talk in numbers, and listen to the data. Intuition, which is to me fundamentally creative, didn't really exist in my mind, or at least I wasn't aware of it yet. I couldn't find it in an equation, so I dismissed the possibility of its existence. Anytime I got that inkling, that little churning in my belly, I either suppressed it or didn't recognize it as intuition. And rightly so! Intuition couldn't be measured in numbers after all, so it had no business taking up residence in my head.

What I've learned by breaking away from the rat-race pace of the career track, and turning off the outcome-fixated auto-pilot I lived with for so long, is something completely different than that concrete and calculating thinking of the hard scientist I was in my youth. I still use that logical side, but I also know now how to work with the less structured material of my intuition. The more I really slow down, meditate, take long walks in nature, and give my feminine energy more space to blossom, the more I understand my intuition. I can now sense my intuition when the signals pop up, and how much better I am at interpreting what it's guiding me to do.

Facts and numbers and science rely on logic. They are cause and effect equations. If you do this thing then that thing happens. Intuition seems to have its own, cryptic chemistry. And it often starts with a feeling that I tune into with questions. Goosebumps cover my arms, or I get a feeling in my stomach, and then I start to relax or ease into the feeling, not trying to force something to occur. I ask, "Okay, what's going on here? What did I just hear, what did I just see that is encouraging my inner wisdom to speak up?" I consciously take my foot off the gas pedal and allow my thoughts to come to a slow idle, softening my focus and allowing an idea to occupy me fully. "What is coming up now?"

It's taken me some time to learn this new practice. At first I read books – a lot of books – in an attempt to pry out some linear step-by-step method I could take to achieve a clearer, cleaner, bullet-pointed guide to receiving my intuition. I was using my left-brain to access my right brain, and this was actually stifling the creative side I was trying to give life to. It was a little like trying to coerce a plant to grow. Counterproductive at best.

Consequently, I had to relinquish some of my assertive point A to point B thinking. I had to shuck off my goal-fixated, aggressive achiever shell. That way, this other, softer aspect could lead me. Simply put, I had to rely on my feminine qualities rather than my masculine qualities. I had to learn to relax, be in flow, and somehow let time stand still so that I could receive.

As I got better at this, I could be in the shower, and then, bam, an intuitive idea would come to me. I could be driving to a client meeting or washing the dishes in the late afternoon sun, my mind wandering after lunch, when a wave of inspiration would fill me. This was my intuition sprouting up through the relaxed and still moments of my life.

As I continued to change the way I lived, I learned to trust my gut more. Rather than rushing from meeting to meeting or phone call to phone call or person to person or crisis to crisis, I began to find a different, less-hurried pace to daily life. It was meditative and relaxed, not that pressured dash that catapulted me forward into some stranded and distant future. I was finding quiet in the moment, even if the moment was loud. And I was actively creating space for me to be intuitive and relaxed during the day. I was actually scheduling time to take walks, listen to music, relax, and meditate. Before this shift, my intuition and inspiration were pushed down, trounced over, and squished, like tiny seedlings under the careening force of a giant tractor wheel. Now, those seedlings are blossoming throughout my day like the intermittent blue flowers on the cascading vine of a Morning Glory.

Chapter 49

Honey Attracts More Flies than Vinegar

I have heard it said, "I'm harder on myself than anyone else is," and that is certainly true for me. For the longest time, I thought that the tendency to push myself was a badge of honor. The critical voice in my head—that voice that would tell me to be better, work harder, study more, get it right, do it perfectly, don't fail, do it again, etc., etc.—I thought that was a good thing. I thought it was my friend. It's true that in many ways, that voice has helped me achieve my goals. It has driven me to some fantastic successes.

I've always earned good grades, I was captain of the sports teams I played on, I progressed in my career to achieve a high level of leadership, and I increased my salary over time. But at what cost did I earn these successes? Considering the harsh coaching of my inner-critic that accompanied me everywhere I went, it was a tough price to pay.

To others it appeared that I had it all. But inside, I never thought I was doing enough. I thought if there was more time I could put into something, I'd be able to attain more. And that next level of achievement I wanted sat just out of reach, like the cookie jar on the top shelf. Shiny, distant, removed. What I failed to see when relying on the goading of this critical voice was just how limiting its words could be.

Rather than being truly content and grateful for my successes, I continually turned outward, looking to others for approval. I was never internally approving of myself, so I needed to hear approval from others. And what's crazy about this is that, though people thought I was successful, I felt like their approval was one of those cookies. Always, forever out of my reach, no matter how I stretched myself to grab hold of it. I felt like I wasn't good enough "yet," like I lacked something essential that would help me get the love and approval I really sought. What a tough predicament I'd invented for myself. The harder I tried and the more I succeeded, the more frustrated I became that I couldn't feel the sense of others' approval I really wanted.

My simple desire to be loved twisted into a painful form of perfectionism, as I believed that each new level of effort could potentially bring me what I sought. It didn't work, of course. These attempts only caused burnout, and the harsh voice urging me to always do better and the fact that my success didn't really bring me closer to others only brought me pain. It shouldn't be a surprise that I now refer to myself as a "recovering perfectionist."

I say "recovering" and not "recovered," because I am still on this journey. I am still learning to practice self-compassion, to acknowledge the progress I am making rather than seeking an unrealistic standard of achievement. (It would be easy for me to be a perfectionist about not being a perfectionist.) I am reminded of something a boss of mine used to say to me all the time. "You can attract more flies with honey than with vinegar," which, in this context, means that my inner critic reaps less successful results than my self-compassionate side does. When I am sweet and self-caring, I actually come closer to creating what I want—the outward successes, and the love, and a sense of belonging.

Self-compassion means being gentle with myself,

even if a decision I make doesn't yield the results I wanted. Self-compassion means allowing so-called mistakes to happen—even loving them! – and making the necessary adjustments with care, when they do. For example, rather than saying to myself, "You should have known better. What's wrong with you?" I can practice self-compassion by acknowledging and validating myself like this: "Given the information you had at the time, it's no wonder you made that decision! It totally makes sense. You were doing the best you could with what you had. Now, what would you like to do to course correct and head in the direction you want to go next?"

This kind of inner-dialogue allows me to take care of myself, while still finding and taking the appropriate action in a given situation. And that's just a start. I have learned many other methods for self-compassion through the help of coach and Zen meditation specialist, Alex Mill.[*]

From Alex, I have learned how to replace that harsh inner voice with a much softer, self-compassionate voice. A voice of love and patience—the very things I was always looking for.

Here are some of his suggestions, which I use on a regular basis:

~ Address the tough inner-voice as a third party... it's not *you* talking, it's a needling, critical voice speaking *to* you. Often this critic even speaks in a way reminiscent of someone we knew or someone we know, such as a teacher, a family member or a partner.

---

[*] For more about self-compassion, check out alexandermilljr.com.

~ Acknowledge and validate the voice. To do this, notice that the voice is actually speaking up to try to protect you from something. The voice thinks you are in danger and that if it doesn't speak up, you will get hurt or disappointed. Accordingly, you should acknowledge that the voice is trying to protect you. Thank it for looking out for you. Send it love and remind it that you are safe. This is what it wants, after all—your safety!

~ Slow down, breathe, and write down what you hear the voice saying. Draw out all the hidden and covert beliefs that underpin this voice. What does the inner critic think about how the world, others, and you should be? How do these ideas lead to the desire to protect you and keep you safe? Once you have these beliefs identified, practice Byron Katie's "The Work" with them. Write them out, ask questions of them, turn them around, and you will see how these beliefs just simply are not true.

~ Record what the voice is saying on your phone or a recording device. Then play it back. When you have some distance from the moment, when you hear the message spoken aloud, you will often perceive it with more objectivity. And from this vantage point, you will be able to see through the spell the voice usually casts over you. Moreover, you will be able to replace its harsh claims and barbed jabs with more love and self-compassion.

~ Consider whether you would speak to a friend in the way the voice is speaking to you. Rarely do we treat others as harshly and judgmentally as we treat ourselves. In fact, often the way we speak to ourselves would sound downright abusive if said out loud to another. For extra impact, ask yourself, "Would I speak this way to a scared child?" Fear, after all, is the motivating force behind the voice, and fear rarely responds well to cutting criticism.

~ Speaking of which, try this method. Think of the voice as a scared little girl (or boy). Reassure the voice that everything is okay. Speak to it softly, sweetly, compassionately and confidently. Then move forward and take constructive action to make the situation better.

These are just a few methods I use to great effect regularly. When you practice being more gentle with yourself, you begin to realize how much kinder the universe actually is to you. You experience life more effortlessly. Compassion is a beautiful gift to give yourself. And, ultimately, it leads to the true success we all want: greater love and kindness!

Chapter 50

Righting the Order of Love

When I reflect back on an experience I had in April of 2010, I remember the five words one of the practitioners said to me... As I thanked her for being a part of my healing scenario, she said, "Thank YOU! By being here and participating, you've helped to RIGHT THE ORDER OF LOVE."

"Right the Order of Love"... How amazing is that?

The event I attended was called a Family Constellation Session. It's an incredible process that is used to heal old wounds and core beliefs that continue to show up as patterns throughout a person's life. I had been in many unhealthy relationships over the years and I wanted to stop the cycle.

Since I was "given away" at birth and put up for adoption by my birth mother, I had thought that this meant that I was not loved or loveable. And this belief carried into so much of my life and fueled the victim energy that told me I was not good enough. It told me I was not worthy of a happy, healthy, relationship with a loving man. I believed that I had to prove myself to others or develop some value that was not inherently in me, that I was fighting an uphill battle to earn love. This was the heart of my approval-seeking tendencies and perhaps my unchecked quest for more and better success. This desperate love-seeking drove me to burnout and struggle.

Through the Family Constellation process, I was finally able to experience and know that I had been conceived in love and came into this world as pure love. This awareness opened up my heart and reconnected me to what I had always been at my core. Pure love. Pure Level 7 (Creator) energy.

This sudden epiphany was liberating! Sheer freedom! Knowing I no longer had to remain victim to my beliefs of unworthiness was true peace. I was no longer trapped in thoughts that I was unloveable. And from there true progress started for me.

It was April 2010 that I had these insights. And major shifts began to happen quickly. As you may recall, I spoke earlier about how much my life had revolved around alcohol. It was June of 2010 when I stopped the excessive drinking. I was also a social smoker, a habit I picked up in college. That also ended in June 2010. And shortly after all that, I began to study coaching and other ways to grow as an individual.

As I was righting the order of love in my own life, things around me, too, began to shift and I seemed to be present for more love in general. I mentioned earlier the "chance" meeting of my son's birthmother on a flight from Detroit to Denver. That was August 2010; the first time she had seen him in person since she had chosen adoption for him ten years earlier.

My journey continues to this day… I am able to live each day working with clients who discover for themselves the pure love that's inside them—always. As my coach continues to help me remove the veil of beliefs I sometimes hold on to that hides that love from view, I get the privilege of helping others, which is another way for me to continue to 'Right the Order of Love'.

And so here I am now, putting my thoughts into these pages, trying to leave you with a greater sense of that love inside you. This is the point I want to emphasize here in the final pages of the book. Love is all around us. Love is in us. It's what we're made of. And each one of us has the option to question the beliefs that obscure it from view.

No matter what story you have, no matter what experiences you've had, how loving or tough your family life, you, my dear one, are like everyone else in this world, and I want you to see that. You are, at your core, pure unconditional love. I'm hoping that by reading this book and using some of its concepts and practices that you will see this reality more and more as you move along on your chosen path.

And the beautiful part of this journey is that there is no destination, only new experiences each day. As John Wooden, one of the most successful basketball coaches of all time said, "Make each day your masterpiece." Make each day and each moment a chance to slow down and right the order of love.

Chapter 51

Slow Dancing with the Universe

Before I learned to slow down, I used to wake up with a question driving my actions. "How do I attack this day?"

Happily, I have replaced that phrase with another, more sustaining, loving, peaceful mantra. I now ask, "How do I slow dance with the universe?"

This question helps me get back into the natural rhythm and pulse of life, back into flow with what is and what can be.

Rather than fighting and trying to wrestle satisfaction from the world, slow dancing becomes a more fulfilling way to have a productive day. It represents the paradox at the core of this book.

As we slow down and ease into the moment, rather than fighting and scraping by, we can thrive as we are meant to. As agents of love.

Here is a little checklist to help you along your path.

The Steps for Your Slow Dance

1. EXPERIMENT: treat your days as laboratories and your choices as experiments leading to what will most fulfill you and serve others. Allow yourself to feel this pressure-free approach.

2. ASK: Who or what can help me move forward? Then go find that support.

3. REFLECT: Throughout the day, ask yourself: Is what I'm doing right now aligned with my core

values? This will help you course correct toward your goals.

4. CHECK-IN: Be kind to yourself, be compassionate. When feeling low, acknowledge and validate yourself, acknowledge the feeling and allow it to be. Don't fight it.

5. QUESTION: Ask yourself how true the belief is... Am I distorting reality? What else could be true?

6. REMEMBER: We always have choices. There are so many possibilities for any given situation or decision. Once we are free from our limiting beliefs, we start to get creative and see how unlimited our options really are.

Chapter 52

My Wish for You

Everything we've talked about, all the skills, tools, stories, perspectives that we've covered in our time together are now a part of who you are. Once you've become aware of them, you can't lose them. The ideas and practices we've covered are always there for you, like the guidance of a good friend, loving, compassionate, understanding.

And I'm glad I had the chance to share with you what has worked for me and my clients, because what I see for you is unbounded. Unbounded opportunity. Unbounded wellness. Unbounded wealth. Unbounded happiness.

It's all right there. All you have to do is slow down and allow your mind to clear. Then you will see the ever present abundance of your life. Right there in front of you, around you, and inside you.

Everything you want is available. And what a wonderful gift that is.

I want to thank you for the courage you've shown in your openness to what we've explored in our time together.

It takes great courage to practice self-compassion and ownership while the world around you continues to provide opportunities to compare yourself to someone else out there. Someone who may seem smarter, stronger, prettier, thinner, wealthier, happier, etc.

It takes great courage to choose to question beliefs that you've held on to for a lifetime.

It takes great courage to look at your life, and then decide you want more.

It takes great courage to test out ideas, concepts, and tools; to be open and willing to see where they take you; to step into the unknown.

YOU are the only one who can play the part of you best! OWN IT! LIVE IT! LOVE IT!

And remember this as you go forward: by slowing down, connecting to your beautiful essence, you will find all the strength, love, wisdom, kindness and joy in you that you will ever need to live life to the fullest and truly thrive!

Recommended Resources

Steve Chandler: All books and audios, especially, *Fearless, Reinventing Yourself, Hands Off Manager,* (www.stevechandler.com)

Byron Katie: *Loving What Is, Who Would You Be Without Your Story,* (www.thework.com)

Richard Carlson and Joseph Bailey: *Slowing Down to the Speed of Life*

Dusan Djukich: *Straight-Line Leadership*

Amy Johnson: *Being Human,* (www.dramyjohnson.com)

Brian Johnson: PN TV Videos, *Philosopher's Notes,* (www.brianjohnson.me)

Michael Neill: *The Space Within,* (www.michaelneill.org)

George Pransky: *The Relationship Handbook*

Jack Pransky: *Parenting from the Heart*

Leslie Sann: *Life Happens,* (www.lesliesann.com)

Bruce D. Schneider: *Energy Leadership*

Tommy Spaulding: *The Heart Led Leader, It's Not Just Who You Know*

iPEC Coaching Certification Program, (www.ipeccoaching.com)

Melissa Ford Coaching, (www.melissafordcoaching.com)

Raechel Anderson Coaching, (www.thesparklingbride.com)

About the Author

Sherry Welsh started out with a degree in Engineering. Although she didn't quite know what to do with it, it provided her with the technical background to begin a twenty-five year career in manufacturing. The experience she gained in her first job in Southampton, PA, set her on a twenty-year career path with Robert Bosch, GmbH. She moved through plants, corporate offices in Germany and the U.S. and ultimately landed in Michigan, where she has lived for the past twenty years. When she left Bosch, she was one of the few women who were in the executive ranks. She was lured away from Bosch to another automotive supplier to be the head of the Global Sales organization responsible for three billion in Sales.

Although the future seemed bright there, the great recession of 2008 came along and knocked her out of the game... temporarily. As a single mom, unemployed in Detroit, Michigan, in one of the greatest recessions of all time, the future seemed bleak. It was during this time that Sherry was able to slow down, set up a consulting practice, and use the skills she had developed over the years as a leader. In that year of consultant work, Sherry discovered her love for coaching and mentoring.

Another company came along, a British Cosmetic packaging company that invited her on a two-year stint as a Global Sales leader. Sherry worked with colleagues around the world again and loved the team she was developing and leading in Paris, Amsterdam, Brazil, New York and Chicago—to name a few locations. Working with customers like Chanel, Christian Dior, and LÓreal was a dream! But due to the nature of the work, every week she was on an airplane, at a different hotel, in a different city. Despite her love for travel, this way of life as a single mom was exhausting.

That's when the Institute for Professional Excellence in Coaching (iPEC) popped up on her radar! It offered exactly what Sherry loved most about working with the multicultural teams she had worked with around the world: inspiring and coaching them to be their best!

Now an independent, professional coach, Sherry works with clients around the world to help them discover and bring their innate leadership abilities into all aspects of their life. She continues to travel and co-parent her incredible son; only now she does so with more humor, a greater sense of ease, and a mind open to a world of possibilities.

To reach Sherry, send her an e-mail:

sherry@sherrywelsh.com

Or visit her website:

www.sherrywelsh.com